Trout Lessons

Trout Lessons

FREEWHEELING TACTICS AND ALTERNATIVE TECHNIQUES
FOR THE DIFFICULT DAYS

Ed Engle

STACKPOLE
BOOKS

Copyright © 2010 by Ed Engle

Published by
STACKPOLE BOOKS
5067 Ritter Road
Mechanicsburg, PA 17055
www.stackpolebooks.com

Printed in China

First edition

10 9 8 7 6 5 4 3 2 1

Illustrations by Tessa J. Sweigert

Library of Congress Cataloging-in-Publication Data

Engle, Ed, 1950–
  Trout lessons : freewheeling tactics and alternative techniques for the difficult days / Ed Engle. — 1st ed.
      p. cm.
  Includes bibliographical references and index.
  ISBN-13: 978-0-8117-0581-3 (hardcover)
  ISBN-10: 0-8117-0581-1 (hardcover)
  1. Trout fishing. 2. Fly fishing. 3. Flies, Artificial. I. Title.
  SH687.E674 2010
799.17'55—dc22
                                        2009038549

CONTENTS

Introduction   vi

CHAPTER 1: Nymphing   1

CHAPTER 2: Attractor Flies   19

CHAPTER 3: Tight-Line Tactics   39

CHAPTER 4: Meadow Streams   67

CHAPTER 5: Catching Difficult Trout   87

CHAPTER 6: High-Water Strategies   105

CHAPTER 7: Small-Stream Finesse   131

CHAPTER 8: Oddities   157

References and Books of Interest   179

Index   181

INTRODUCTION

My intentions when I started writing *Trout Lessons* were pretty straightforward. The plan was to give fly fishers some ideas for those days on the river when the usual stuff didn't work. I envisioned a practical guide directed toward specific situations, such as what to do if you're getting refusal rises to a fly pattern that the trout had been perfectly happy to take the day before under the same conditions. I hoped to examine a number of cases where the usual tactics had failed and then supply a checklist of possible technical solutions. I also wanted to discuss what to do if the river itself wasn't acting normally. The most obvious example of that would be a river that is disastrously high and muddy with runoff. I should say I use the word "disastrously" here not so much from the river's or even the trout's point of view, but more from the point of view of a disappointed fly fisher whose expectations have been crushed.

When I look back now, I can say that I actually did accomplish what I initially set out to do. To be sure, there is the section on some techniques to try when the river is dirty and ideas for those days when the trout seem uncooperative for no good reason. There are also some interesting tips on using familiar fly patterns or techniques in unusual ways. But the biggest surprise in *Trout Lessons* for me was what emerged in addition to what I set out to do. As I gathered and wrote down alternative techniques to use when the usual fly-fishing tactics failed, I found that my own tactics weren't as usual as I had thought.

I come from a generation of fly fishers who embraced technical solutions to angling problems. We believed that if you were observant and matched the size, color, and silhouette of an insect that the trout were eating and then skillfully presented that imitation to a trout in a way that made it appear like the real thing, you would catch the trout. I still believe that, and I think most fly fishers would agree that, to use the buzzwords, matching the hatch and a drag-free drift probably account for more trout hookups than any other fly-fishing method.

But that doesn't mean that matching the hatch is the only way to catch a trout or that it has always been the prevailing fly-fishing strategy. Many years ago John Betts, who among his many fly-fishing talents is very knowledgeable about the sport's history, told me that there appear to be historical cycles where fly fishermen wholeheartedly embrace the more scientific match-the-hatch philosophy and then on the other end of the cycle embrace more freewheeling attractor fly philosophies. The idea that there is no single path to fly-fishing success and that some of our most deeply held fly-fishing beliefs may be affected by cyclical trends has always stuck with me.

When I was researching *Trout Lessons* I found myself more closely examining the way I fly-fish. I realized that I wasn't always the hard-core match-the-hatch, drag-free-drift fly fisherman I thought I was. It started when I noticed how often I purposely added a little bit of a decidedly non-drag-free lift to the end of a dead drift and got a strike. But what I found more interesting was that even though I understood that the strike was probably induced by the lift, it took me years to recognize that subtle tight-line tactics had, paradoxically, become part of my everyday drag-free drift philosophy.

I wouldn't say that because I sometimes use a lift, pull a dry fly under the water on purpose, or dead-drift a nymph on an "almost" tight line I am radically departing from currently accepted fly-fishing practice. But what I did finally understand while writing *Trout Lessons* was that I needed to consciously include thinking outside of the match-the-hatch, drag-free-drift box into my everyday fly-fishing strategy—if only because it opens a whole new realm of possibilities for catching difficult trout.

I think that when you read *Trout Lessons* you will indeed find the intended technical suggestions for what to do when the usual tactics fail; but I also hope the book will go one step further and encourage you to let go of any preconceived fly-fishing notions you may have and ultimately allow the trout and

the river to inform you about the best solution to a given fly-fishing problem.

So with that in mind, I hope that the next time you discover a decidedly non-technical solution to, let's say, a fly-fishing problem on a small mountain stream that it won't just end there, but you'll find a way to apply it or elements of it to a very technical problem on a spring creek the next year. That, to my way of thinking, would be total fly fishing.

A lot of people have helped make this book possible. I owe a special debt of gratitude to the fly-fishing magazine editors who over the years have supported me by regularly publishing my articles. Portions of some of the chapters in *Trout Lessons* appeared in different, shorter versions in *American Angler*, *Flyfishing & Tying Journal*, and *Fly Fisherman*. Editing a fly-fishing magazine can at times be a thankless, but absolutely necessary, job. Phil Monahan, Dave Hughes, Kim Koch, and John Randolph have all improved my articles through their editorial skill and broadened my horizons both as a writer and fly fisher. Although Jim Babb, the editor at *Gray's Sporting Journal*, wasn't directly involved with any of the chapters in this book, his editorial skills and advice have made me a better writer.

Stackpole Books published my first fly-fishing book and every one that has come after it. The support of both David Detweiler and Judith Schnell at Stackpole has made everything possible. Amy Lerner and the other staff members at Stackpole make me look a lot better than I deserve to.

It has been my good fortune to fish and tie flies with a number of talented, insightful, and articulate anglers over the years. I would understand a lot less about the ways of trout if it weren't for John Gierach, A. K. Best, Gary Anderson, Roy Palm, Jon Kent, Dusty Sprague, Bernard Ramanauskas, Angus Drummond, Ben Brown, Jackson Streit, and Kyle Hendricks.

In terms of technical support, this book would not be possible without the photographic contributions of Angus Drummond, Kyle Hendricks, and Dave Wolverton. Entomologist/fly fisher/author Rick Hafele, as is always the case, came to my rescue when I needed answers to entomological questions. Master fly tier Chris Helm supplied technical know-how for spinning deer hair and quality fly-tying materials. Debra Rose's illustrations of trout riseforms added to and enhanced the text.

I would be remiss to not recognize the people that I've guided on the South Platte River over the past twenty years. Their support has allowed me to spend time on the water and make the kind of observations that are the key to any fly-fishing book. Although most of my fishing guests might not believe it, I learn as much as they do every time we're on the river. I should also say that it would not be possible for me to guide at all without the help, support, and friendship of Tony Gibson and Colorado Fishing Adventures.

Finally, I would like to thank Eric Ishiwata, Rick Takahashi, Glenn Weisner, Wayne Samson, Dan Quatro, Charlie Craven, Rick Murphy, and Stan Benton for contributing their fly patterns and advice in *Trout Lessons*.

So many people have offered helpful insights during the preparation of this book that I'm bound to have left out the names of a few contributors. If you are one of them, please accept my thanks for your help.

On a more personal note, I'd like to thank my sweetheart, Jana Rush, who always finds time to copyedit, help illustrate a chapter, or run up to the river with me to take photos. I know a lot of people in the fly-fishing business, and we all agree it ain't easy being our spouses. And it's even harder when we're trying to write a book. I'll finish by acknowledging the unending support that my sister, Carolyn Reyes, and my mother, Bernice Engle, have always given me on my fly-fishing projects—no matter how quirky they appear to be.

CHAPTER 1

Nymphing

Developing a feel for the strike in fast water and slow

It's midmorning on the South Platte River, and the action is clearly below the surface. For this river, at this time of the year, that's not a big surprise. The guides have dutifully provided their clients with the standard Rocky Mountain guide's two-fly, short-line, dead-drifting nymphing rig. And I don't blame them for turning to the rig. Nymphing accounts for more hookups on heavily pressured western tailwaters than all the other fly-fishing techniques combined. Most of the guides probably had the rods pre-rigged for nymphing and hanging from a rack in their Suburban before they even picked their clients up. I don't blame them for that either because most of us know what flies the trout will eat, and having the rods rigged saves time on the water.

I'll do everything pretty much the same way for my fishing guest today, with one exception: I always rig the rods up when I'm on the river. That doesn't mean that I won't put on the exact same flies that I would have put on back at the truck or even at home the night before the trip. I just like walking down to the river, standing by it, and talking about how we think the day should go. I can't say that my motives were always this pure. Twenty years ago I used to rig my fishermen up on the water so that I could hold the location. I was new to guiding then and only knew four or five places on the river where I could consistently put a fisherman on trout. My lack of confidence always made me anxious to get to one of my spots before the other guides or recreational anglers did. It wasn't uncommon then or even now to actually see a fisherman race to a spot just because he *thought* another angler was heading to it.

After a number of guide seasons, I began to realize there was a lot of water on the

Since its popularization in the 1970s, short-line dead-drift nymphing has gained a steady stream of converts among fly fishers. A seemingly infinite number of variations of the technique have evolved since that time.

river that held trout. Most of it wasn't the kind of deep, fishbowl guide holes where you could park an angler all day because it held fifty trout. This was more subtle water that ran through a little trough or twist that dependably held four or five trout. It was the kind of water most fishermen walk right by. I also realized that it just wasn't worth racing anyone for a spot on the river. Whether you're guiding or just out for a day of pleasure fishing, you have to always believe that you can find trout and take some risks to make it happen. That's as much a part of fishing as the inevitable new fly rod.

Anyway, on this day, right now on the river, I am in fact going to rig my fisherman up with the standard two-fly nymphing rig. We're starting off with a gray goose biot midge larvae imitation that I know is pretty deadly this time of year. I've tied it in the point position with a flashy Barr Emerger knock-off about fifteen inches from it in the dropper position, although I will actually tie the emerger directly into the leader rather than dangle it off a true dropper. I'll also have to add some weight ten inches up the leader from the Barr knock-off because the flies are too small to be weighted themselves. How much weight I attach to the leader is important. It needs to be just enough to get the flies down to the bottom, but not so much that the current can't bounce it downstream in a natural fashion. Theoretically, if I set this up right, the artificial flies will dead-drift downstream in a way that's natural enough to give the illusion of a real nymph, pupa, or larva that has inadvertently gotten kicked into the drift, or perhaps a nymph or pupa that is starting its dangerous journey to the water's surface where it will emerge into a

Basic short-line nymphing technique is achieved by holding as much fly line off the water as possible.

As the flies drift downstream, follow the drift with the rod tip.

Continue to follow the drift until the flies begin to drag.

winged, air-breathing adult. The final element of the rig will be a strike indicator. In this case I'm attaching a small, hard foam indicator at a distance that equals the depth of the water plus two feet above the weight.

If you've fished with me before, none of this is new, but I always go over the setup while I'm rigging it. If you are familiar with nymphing, you'll know that there are an almost infinite number of variations to a two-fly nymphing rig. You can change the position of the weight or alter where you put the strike indicator. Your choice of the strike indicator itself can be anything from a piece of yarn to a puny little half-inflated balloon. Some nymphers add a third fly imitation. You can use a weighted fly rather than a split shot or substitute tungsten putty. It goes on and on, but in the end, no matter how you rig it, the principle of the technique is the same. You are trying to get the flies down to where the trout will see them in such a way that they appear and behave like the real thing.

After the rigging ritual I position my fisherman in a nice run, and since he is an experienced nympher we only briefly review how to high-stick a nymph on a short line. I mention that the key is to cast far enough upstream to allow the weight to pull the flies to the bottom before they get into the strike zone, which in this case is pretty easy to determine since we can see trout suspended and feeding in three feet of water about fifteen feet from us. I remind my guest that as his flies are drifting downstream toward the trout he should follow the strike indicator's progress with the rod tip and lift the rod higher to take up the slack line. Once the flies and indicator are downstream from him he needs to lower the fly rod to add more slack line, which will extend the drift.

Finally, I admonish him to keep only enough line out to get the job done, which

Beginning nymph fishermen often have trouble with the water tension cast used to flip the flies back upstream when the drift is complete. The key to executing the water tension cast is to allow the current to lift the weighted flies to the surface on a tight line before you begin the cast. PHOTO BY ANGUS DRUMMOND

Once the current lifts the flies to the surface and they are trailing downstream of you, lift the fly rod to the one o'clock position. This lifts most of the fly line off the water to facilitate the cast. PHOTO BY ANGUS DRUMMOND

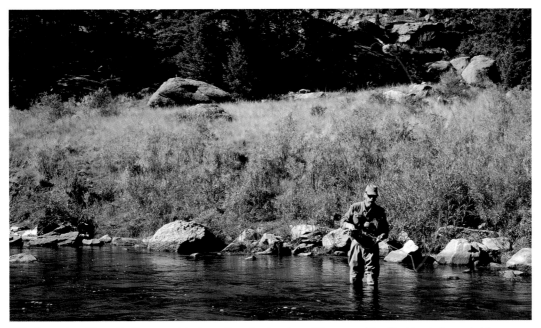

With the rod positioned in the one o'clock position, the tension of the current in effect loads the rod. All you need to do is apply the power stroke in much the same way as you would on a roll cast to launch the flies back upstream. PHOTO BY ANGUS DRUMMOND

in this case is the leader and about four feet of fly line past the rod tip. Other than that we briefly go over the tension or water cast that nymphers use to flip the rig back upstream. I tell him to remember to let the current pull the flies to the surface at the end of the drift before he uses the tension of the current to load the rod and flip the flies upstream in a way that is similar to a roll cast. He knows from experience that the key to this cast is to raise the fly rod to the one or two o'clock position before making the power stroke that sends the flies and weight winging upstream. Raising the rod like that lifts the line off the water and makes the cast easier and more accurate.

So we go to work. The drifts are good enough to get a strike, but lack what I call the "concentration" that's necessary to refine the subsurface presentation. What I mean by concentration goes beyond the angler's own mental concentration to include all the elements in a short-line nymphing presentation that are necessary to optimize success. These elements include line management, rod management, fly management, and mental concentration. It doesn't take too many more drifts before I begin to see what in recent years has become a subtle but familiar pattern among the anglers I take fishing. The weirdest thing is that on the surface everything looks right. The fisherman is allowing the flies to get to the bottom, he's mending the strike indicator upstream whenever necessary to keep it over or upstream of where he imagines the flies to be as they drift downstream, and he's following the drift with the rod tip. What he isn't doing is staying in contact with the fly. Or, put another way, it's the dreaded curse of the strike indicator.

THE FOTHERGILL NYMPHING TECHNIQUE

Let's roll the clock back to the early 1970s when I learned to short-line nymph-fish in the Cheesman Canyon section of the South Platte River. Although a few fly fishers were using primitive strike indicators at the time, the majority of us were unknowing disciples of a modified form of Chuck Fothergill's outrigger nymphing method. Fothergill described his method as an "upstream, deaddrift, tight-line, high-rod, weighted-nymph technique" in the 1979 anthology, *The Masters on the Nymph*, edited by J. Michael Migel and Leonard M. Wright Jr. He said that Lefty Kreh had once referred to the method as the "outrigger technique" because Fothergill's habit of holding the rod high made it look like an outrigger and the name had stuck. As it turned out the name didn't really stick but was ultimately supplanted by the more inclusive term, "high-sticking." We just called it short-line nymphing at the time.

Although Fothergill's original outrigger method used longer casts than the short-line tactics that evolved on the South Platte, Frying Pan, and other rivers, the goal of both techniques was to prevent drag by holding as much fly line as possible off the water's surface. What interested us most about shortline and outrigger tactics was that weight was used to get the nymph imitation down to the stream bottom where the trout were actually feeding. The technique had clear advantages over the then-popular tactic of swinging a weighted nymph across and downstream like you fished a wet fly. Unfortunately, the imitation seldom sank deep enough to get into the trout's feeding zone. The revolutionary short-line and outrigger

The classic Fothergill outrigger nymphing technique relies on casting a slightly longer line. The connection between the leader and fly line is used as a strike detector.

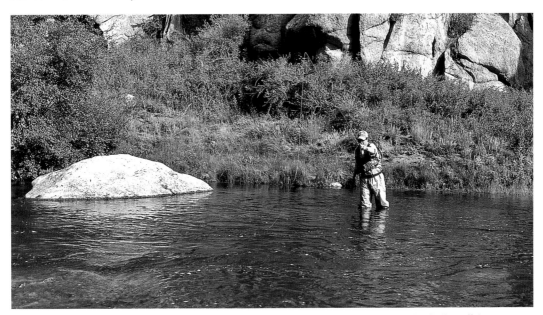

Short-line nymphing techniques modified Fothergill's outrigger method by holding all the fly line off the water whenever possible and watching where the leader intersected the water or using a strike indicator to detect strikes.

nymphing tactics were highly productive and within a few years became some of the most effective, popular, and controversial ways to fly-fish for trout.

Fothergill's technique was executed by casting a weighted nymph across and up-stream and then allowing it to drift drag-free downstream. To accomplish this you had to cast close in and then hold the rod high and follow the drift of the nymph downstream with the rod tip. The key was to have as little slack leader (or in rare cases slack line and leader) on the water as possible as your nymph imitation bounced and tumbled along the stream bottom. Holding the rod high and following the drift downstream with the rod tip allowed you to do this.

THE ALMOST TIGHT LINE

Unless you read very carefully this sounds pretty much like the way fly-fishing writers and guides have been describing the various incarnations of short-line nymphing with or without a strike indicator for the past thirty years. And it is a very good descrip-tion as long as you don't forget the way Fothergill originally phrased it. He de-scribed it as an "upstream, dead-drift, *tight-line*, high-rod, weighted-nymph" technique. I've added the emphasis to tight-line be-cause that's a crucial detail that nymphers have forgotten. The early descriptions of the various short-line, dead-drift nymphing techniques instructed beginners to watch the leader/fly line connection or where the leader entered the water or, best of all, the fish itself to detect strikes. But that was really only a starting point. The more per-ceptive nymphers realized that if they kept the line just a hair shy of tight and guided

the flies as they drifted downstream that they could feel strikes.

This was new territory when it came to detecting strikes. A strike wasn't totally tactile like when a trout hit a streamer fished on the swing, but it wasn't purely visual strike detec-tion either. It was a combination of watching the leader or the line *and* being perceptive to the subtle changes that can indicate a strike on a tight line. Some nymphers who picked up on detecting subtle strikes by feel actually got to the point where they relied less and less on visual cues. Other nymphers who practiced good technique may not have even realized that they were relying on detecting strikes by feel. They were sometimes dumb-founded when they somehow just *knew* to set the hook and discovered a trout was on. Some of them even considered it a kind of mystical gift, but the more likely reason for their success was they were maintaining the line just shy of tight because they believed it was facilitating a dead drift. It turns out it was also helping them detect strikes even if it was a close to subliminal sense.

Lazy nymphers like me took it a step fur-ther. While some nymphers were spending half their time changing weight and rigs every time they moved to a new run, I just kept the same amount of weight on unless conditions changed radically. If my flies were hanging up on the bottom in a slower-moving run, I simply lifted the rod tip and helped or led the flies through the run by applying just a bit more tension on the leader. If the water was a little deeper or faster, I cast farther upstream to allow the flies more time to get to the bottom. Although I didn't know it at the time, when I led my flies through the run I was employing a fundamental principle

When short-line nymphing without a strike indicator, maintaining an almost tight line aids in detecting subtle strikes.

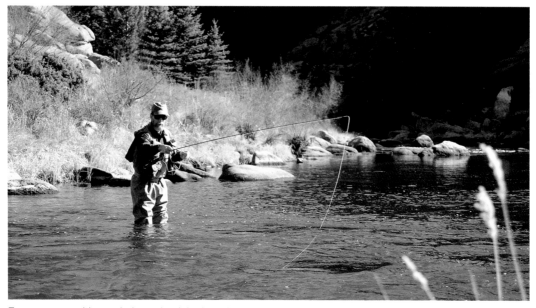

European nymphing techniques lead the heavily weighted nymphs through a run on a tight line or almost tight line. PHOTO BY KYLE HENDRICKS

of what the European tournament nymphers in the 1980s eventually coined as Czech or Polish nymphing. And, at the time, so were a lot of other nymph fishermen.

That's why I was surprised when Czech nymphing hit the scene in the United States and everyone thought it was such a new, radical way to nymph. But then I realized what had happened. When I learned to nymph in the 1970s, none of us used strike indicators, so we had to learn how to detect subtle strikes by feel. When strike indicators eventually became popular, we incorporated them into our nymphing rigs because they did help us visually detect strikes. But we never lost our sixth sense of detecting strikes by feel. At least in the early days of strike indicators, it was easy enough to maintain that sixth sense because the first strike indicators were little more than the addition of a brightly colored tag to the leader or the fly line tip. Some nymphers painted their leader knots in highly visible fluorescent colors. Others threaded a 1-inch long section of orange fly line into the leader. The idea was that it would be easier to detect strikes by watching the brightly colored indicator than watching the sometimes difficult to see leader/water interface. And since the indicators didn't really float, we still had to keep our casts short and fish a tight line to get a good drift.

BUOYANT STRIKE INDICATORS

The introduction of buoyant strike indicators changed all of that. Buoyant strike indicators actually floated like corks (the first ones really were corks), and nymphers quickly adapted to them. Most often they employed a kind of hybrid short-line rig where the buoyant indicator was placed one-and-a-half

times the depth of the water above the weighted fly or the weight attached to the leader. The extra leader length between the weight and strike indicator was a hedge against the drag that was bound to occur if the indicator was set at the depth of the water. The extra slop allowed the angler to prevent drag by mending just the indicator upstream while the weighted fly continued its drift along the bottom. The good news was that strikes were easier to detect, the bad news was that the slack caused a delay in the detection time that could result in a missed strike or a foul-hooked fish. And there was one other more subtle change. Nymph fishermen began to lose physical contact with their flies. Strike detection was becoming all visual.

From the point of view of most guides the buoyant strike indicator was a godsend because the technique allowed them to get clients with little or no fly-fishing experience into trout in a relatively short time. A client could be placed in a run that was known to hold a lot of trout and then taught to master the drift in that one location. When it came to detecting strikes, it didn't matter if the client was late or even missed a bunch of strikes because he'd certainly hook up on at least a few fish. Although this may sound like a restrictive day of angling to experienced fly fishers, it certainly helped get novices into trout, which is part of a guide's job, and that successful first fly-fishing experience might motivate the client to explore the sport in all its nuances. It wasn't all bad.

Things get a little more complicated when you talk about experienced nymphers using buoyant strike indicators. No doubt, a buoyant strike indicator makes long-line

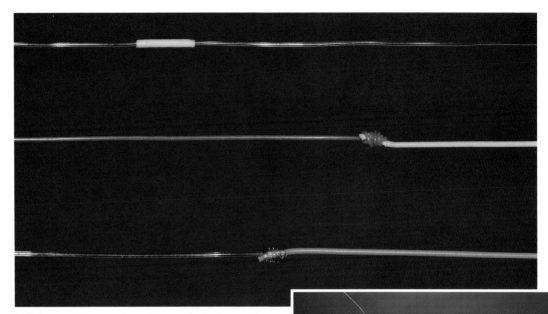

Initially, nymphers used non-buoyant indicators such as (from top), an orange piece of fly line slipped over the leader, a brightly colored Amnesia leader butt section, or simply an orange fly line to help detect strikes.

Buoyant strike indicators can suspend a nymph imitation off the stream bottom. They made strike detection easier and long-line nymphing possible. The buoyant indicators also made strike detection almost totally a visual endeavor.

nymphing practical. It's one of only a few techniques where you can cast a long line and still get close to a drag-free drift. That's because the buoyant indicator acts to suspend the fly just enough to allow a successful drift. As it turns out, the best of all worlds would be to learn to short-line nymph-fish using no-indicator techniques that help develop the touch that is the basis of advanced nymphing practice; once those skills are present then, if necessary or desired, add the

buoyant indicator to the rig. In this way fishermen would develop the critical ability to detect a strike by feel and maintain that sense more easily once the buoyant indicator is employed.

That's where my generation of nymph fishers differs from many current nymphers. We all had some exposure to detecting strikes by feel simply because it was hard not to feel a strike once in a while when nymphing without an indicator. When the buoyant

Buoyant strike indicators made long-line nymphing possible.

indicator appeared, the appeal was almost universal. Everyone switched to them. It didn't take too much practice to get a good drift, and the buoyant indicator really did help detect more strikes than just *watching* a non-buoyant indicator. More fastidious nymphers who were willing to constantly adjust a buoyant indicator could actually suspend a weighted fly just off the stream bottom or at any level in the water column where the trout were holding. That kind of suspension rig made detecting strikes easier because there wasn't a weight bouncing on the stream bottom between the trout's strike and the indicator. Another way of looking at it is that a suspension rig gives you a tight line at least between the indicator and the fly.

What's interesting now is that we have a couple of generations of nymphers who have only learned to detect strikes by watching a buoyant strike indicator. That's why they are so fascinated by the highly effective European tight-line techniques where you feel and see the strike through the line. And that's a step in the right direction because if you want to move to the next level of nymphing, you will need to develop your facility for detecting strikes through the line. I like to think of it as developing *your* lateral line.

Most fly fishers know that many fish species have what is called a lateral line. It's used to detect danger, find prey, and in the case of schooling fish keep them from bumping into each other when the school turns. A fish's lateral line is unlike any of our human senses. I've heard it described as a "long distance sense of feel." The trout in effect feels you when you're wading carelessly because your movements create a pressure change that is transferred through the water

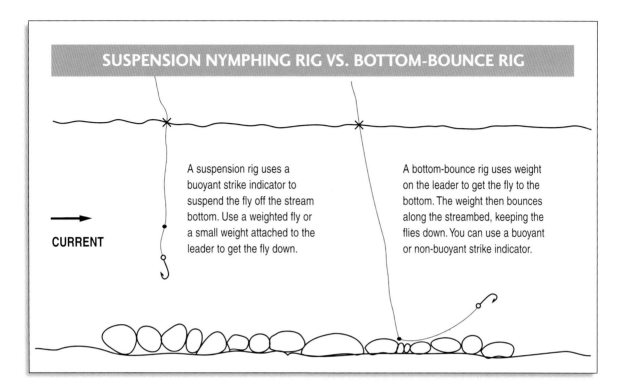

to its lateral line. You can apply the same idea of a long distance sense of feel if you consider the leader and fly line as your own lateral line that when properly tuned allows you to almost instantaneously detect strikes. The key to developing your lateral line is the tight line. Or more precisely, the just shy of a tight line. And the way that you achieve that almost tight line is through fly-rod technique. It's what the guide forgot to talk about when he was hammering on you to watch the strike indicator and yelling, "Strike! Strike! Strike!" every time it moved a smidgen this way or that.

FLY-ROD TECHNIQUE FOR NYMPHING
Good rod technique is the basis for controlling the tension of the leader as the nymph bumps its way along the stream bottom. The

best way to understand this is to consider the anatomy of a short-line nymphing presentation. Typically the cast is made across and upstream with a weighted nymph or a weight attached to the leader. When the weighted nymph first hits the water, it takes time to sink to the bottom. This sink time will vary depending on the depth of the water and current speed.

As a rule, the deeper the water or the faster the current, the farther upstream you'll need to cast to allow the nymph to get to the bottom by the time it enters the strike zone. An alternative to casting farther upstream is to change to a more heavily weighted fly or add more weight to the leader, which will allow you to cast a shorter distance upstream with the same effect. The strike zone begins when the weighted fly drifts downstream

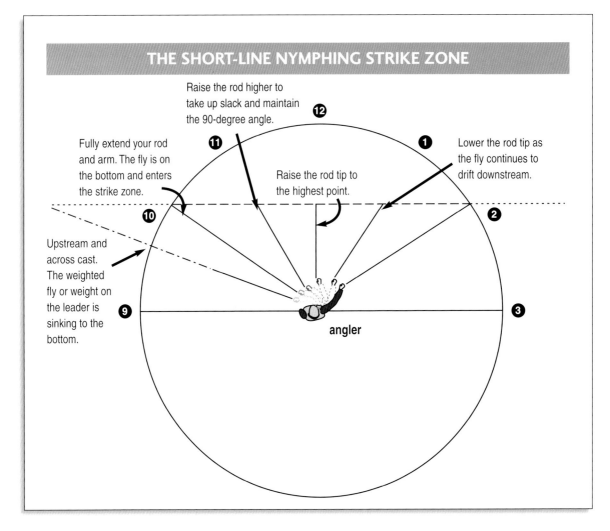

THE SHORT-LINE NYMPHING STRIKE ZONE

Raise the rod higher to take up slack and maintain the 90-degree angle.

Fully extend your rod and arm. The fly is on the bottom and enters the strike zone.

Raise the rod tip to the highest point.

Lower the rod tip as the fly continues to drift downstream.

Upstream and across cast. The weighted fly or weight on the leader is sinking to the bottom.

angler

to the point that you can hold the rod tip directly over it. At that point the leader should then be at close to a 90-degree angle to the water. It ends at the point downstream when you can no longer maintain the 90-degree angle while holding the rod tip directly over the fly. This doesn't mean that you won't get a strike when the flies get to the bottom a little farther upstream or drift a bit farther downstream. In fact, as you gain more experience, the odds are that your strike zone will expand. The strike zone just represents the area where you will most easily be able to detect a strike by feel.

You can visualize the strike zone by imagining that you are standing in the center of a large clock with an hour hand that's about the length of your fly rod plus your fully extended arm. The strike zone begins when the hour hand is at about ten and ends when it's at two (see diagram). As the fly drifts through the strike zone, you raise

USING THE ROD TO DIRECT THE DRIFT
AROUND THE NEAR SIDE OF A ROCK

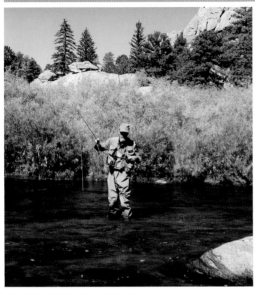

1 Dead-drift the nymph into the prime holding water in front of the rock.

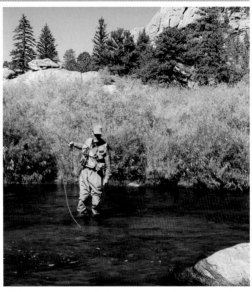

3 Once the nymph is in position to drift around the rock, continue the dead drift.

2 Use the rod and a tight line to direct the drift around the near side of the rock.

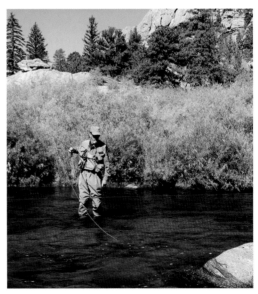

4 Continue the drift around the entire perimeter of the rock.

PHOTOS BY ANGUS DRUMMOND

the rod to take up slack and maintain the 90-degree angle until it reaches the twelve o'clock position. At that point, you lower the rod as the drift continues away from you to the two o'clock position.

Maintaining this 90-degree angle at the leader/water interface gives you close to complete contact with the fly. There is virtually no slack leader on the water, and you are compensating for the current by following the fly's drift downstream with the rod tip. This allows you to quickly sense a strike or when the fly gets hung up on streambed rubble. And believe me, you will get hung up on the bottom plenty, especially in the beginning. You can learn to walk your rig over the obstruction and continue the drift by lifting the rod tip a bit while still maintaining close to a dead drift.

If the weighted fly or weight you've added to the leader is just a bit too heavy, which is by far preferable to being a bit too light, you may find that you have to lead the drift just a little. That simply means that you'll move your rod downstream just a bit faster than the current to prevent the flies from hanging up, and when necessary walk the fly over or around any obstructions with a mini-lift or two.

Finally, don't be afraid to use the rod to help direct the drift around in-stream rocks or adjust a drift to exactly where it needs to be. Initially, some nymphers are hesitant to try this because so much emphasis is placed on the dead drift that they believe any momentary adjustment that disrupts it will ruin the entire drift. And make no mistake, you will actually be ruining the dead drift for that moment or two when you make a mini-lift or adjust a drift, but the re-

wards will far outweigh the disruption of the drift.

DETECTING STRIKES

The traditional advice for detecting strikes when high-sticking a short line without a strike indicator is to watch the leader and water interface or, if you have a little more line out as Chuck Fothergill originally recommended, to watch the fly line and leader connection. If the leader or fly line and leader connection stops, hesitates, or does anything unusual, you set the hook. What they don't tell you is to consider holding the fly line in your line hand rather than clamping it down against the cork with your rod hand. This, at least when you're learning to nymph, enhances your sense of feel and adds it to your sense of sight, which is already watching the leader and water interface for strikes. The increased sensitivity will often allow you to feel strikes before you ever see them, and you'll immediately sense when a streambed obstruction is impeding the fly's drift.

This was the way nymphers fished a short line before strike indicators became popular. Of course, there were variations. Most notably, some experienced nymphers felt they could feel strikes just as well by holding the fly line against the rod's cork handle with their forefinger, and by doing so they could extend out over the water a bit farther to increase the effective range of the strike zone. Once buoyant strike indicators came on the scene, more and more nymphers switched to a totally visual strike detection system where they simply watched the strike indicator bob downstream to detect strikes. That's also about when guides began to focus on teaching beginners to hold the fly line against the

TWO WAYS TO HOLD THE FLY LINE
WHEN SHORT-LINE DEAD-DRIFT NYMPHING

Holding the fly in your line hand may give you a better feel for strikes when short-line dead-drift nymphing.

Holding the fly line against the cork handle of the fly rod when short-line nymphing may diminish your sense of feel when detecting strikes.

rod handle to simplify the technique. The simplification is a good thing, but it also made it more difficult for beginners to develop any sense of feel when it came to detecting strikes.

Almost all of the high-sticking short-line nymphing styles are most effective when used in slow- to moderately fast-moving water up to four or five feet in depth. Although an experienced high-stick nympher can hold his own in heavier water, the European nymphing styles may have some advantages. The European style emphasizes three very heavy, larger, streamlined nymph patterns that are designed to sink quickly and stay on the bottom. You typically lead the flies through the run at a speed slightly faster than the current to prevent them from hanging up on the bottom and to create a tight line to facilitate strike detection in heavier water. Another important variation is that you hold the fly rod tip down close to the water's surface as you lead the flies downstream. This also enhances your ability to feel a strike because you are guaranteed a tight line between you and the strike, whereas any inattention when high-sticking can allow slack to creep in. Finally, the European nymphing leader is typically untapered and seldom uses leader material larger than 4X. The logic here is that you don't really need a tapered leader when you're casting heavily weighted flies (which is actually true for any nymphing rig using weight) and that the lighter material may offer less resistance in the water, which allows the flies to sink more quickly.

In some ways it was, once again, the guides who first embraced the European nymphing system because it's easy to teach a beginning client and, if properly executed, takes a lot of the guesswork out of strike detection. The important thing to remember, no matter what systems you employ, is that developing the ability to feel a strike can result in a quantum leap in your success on the water.

So does this all mean you should throw away your strike indicators? Not at all. There are some applications, such as long-line nymphing techniques, where some sort of floating indicator that suspends the flies is crucial to success. And a buoyant strike indicator can increase your short-line nymphing success too. But if you want to move to the next level of nymphing expertise, you may want to start training your own lateral line by simply taking the strike indicator off once in a while and practicing a few no-indicator techniques. It won't be easy at first, especially if you've been a visual nympher, but if you stick with it, you'll become a better nymph fisherman. You'll learn that you can feel a lot more through the fly line than you ever thought possible when it comes to detecting strikes.

The idea that you can feel or even get a sense of a strike that goes beyond feeling is just one more tool to keep you in the game when the normal stuff isn't working. More than anything, it's a way to adjust your thinking to where you're more open to the most subtle cues on the river. Maybe it's feeling a strike through the fly line or just acting on instinct. But whatever it is, it's a way to get on a razor-thin edge that you didn't think existed. It's that place between a totally visual way of fishing and the tight line world of a swinging wet fly or streamer. It's a place where you have to develop a different sense of things. It's where you're going to need a lateral line. . . .

CHAPTER 2

Attractor Flies

Matching the fly to the water type and activating the fly

The beaver ponds weren't exactly secret, but they were a bit hard to get to. I'd spent the morning backpacking into them with the intention of spending a few days, although a day trip was possible. You could make the two-and-a-half-hour hike early, fish for the better part of the day, and then hike out toward evening, but that meant either making the two-hour drive home that night or just camping by the truck. I figured if I was going to end up camping by the truck anyway, I might as well just pack a bare-bones kit up to the ponds. That meant a single fly box, rod, reel, lightweight stocking foot hippers, wading boots, and my standard backpacking stuff.

One item included in the standard backpacking stuff I carry to new campsites is a cheap pie rack. It's the kind they sell at grocery stores for a few bucks. I use the pie racks for campfire grills and have hidden ten or twelve of them at various backcountry fishing campsites over the years. There was actually one already hidden where I was headed, and I wondered if the bears might have discovered it. Over the years they've found a few at my other campsites but left them in surprisingly good condition if you consider what a bear is capable of. In most cases I've found the grill, licked clean as whistle, within a radius of twenty or thirty feet of my old camp. It almost makes me wonder if the bears somehow intuit that I will return and add another tasty coating of brook trout skin to it. It's all part of this ritual I make out of having a trout dinner or two when I'm up in brookie country. I tell myself that it saves the weight of packing in a few dinners, but more important it is a ritual of trust that the trout will take care of me. I like to remind myself that no matter how many trout I catch and

Brook trout can be plentiful in more remote areas.

release, fishing is still a blood sport. Just ask the trout that's running for its life on the end of your line if you don't believe me. Besides, the Colorado Division of Wildlife practically begs fishermen to eat some brookies in this area because the fishery is overpopulated.

So anyway, I found the grill unmolested where I'd hidden it the year before and quickly set up camp on a little wooded ridge. I then headed straight to the fishing. The beaver ponds are well established, and I could see a few fish rising or swirling in a couple of them. I knew that one pond was deeper than the others and some larger trout were in it, but I decided to get warmed up on a shallower pond that probably held smaller fish. Probably is the right word to use here because I am a fisherman and I always believe that I can be fooled by the water. I have caught some seriously large trout from water that probably held smaller fish.

My fly box was understandably well stocked with the kind of flies that fishermen call attractors: Royal Coachman Trudes, Royal Coachmen, H & L Variants, Lime-Bodied Coachmen. They are flies that don't imitate anything, but imitate everything. They are the kind of flies that you cast to dumb trout like brookies or the less sophisticated trout in faraway places that hardly ever see a fly. I picked the size 12 Royal Coachman Trude because it had been the fly the brookies preferred the year before. It wasn't that fish didn't take the other attractors that I threw at them, they just seemed to pay a bit more attention to this pattern. That sense was amplified in my mind because trout in other locations had seemed to pay more attention to the Trude too.

I didn't have any doubt that I'd get a strike or eventually catch a fish. The drama was whether I'd pull the trigger too soon, causing me to flub the first strike and how many trout I'd land before I put the rest of them down. I lucked out when a nice 7-incher attacked the fly, hooked himself (I say himself because of the little kype), and I managed to land him. I didn't keep this particular fish because brookies in a place like this hold the promise of abundance, and you always figure you can wait until the end of the day before you go to the grocery store. I should, however, say that I've gone hungry before when I depended on the promise of abundance, but of all the fish I angle for in Colorado the brookies most often keep that promise.

You will recognize some additional details about the attractor fly. I chose a large one for the beaver ponds in hopes that it would deter some of the 5-inch and smaller brookies, but this was with full knowledge that it often doesn't. The size 12 Royal Coachman Trude fits the idea of an attractor fly pattern like a glove. It's large, utilizes the color red, and employs peacock herl, which is a required secret ingredient. In addition, it has a bushy calftail wing tied trude-style and plenty of brown hackle. And don't forget the tail. It could just as well be brown hackle fibers, but this fly has golden pheasant tippet tails just in case the other stuff isn't attractive enough.

It's not all about being gaudy either, although the word or a similar one comes up often when the conversation turns to attractor flies. This fly really does work in all kinds of situations. The techie fly-fishing guys will sit you down and carefully explain that the two bumps of peacock make it look like an ant or the red floss reminds the brookie of

MATCHING THE HATCH

Match-the-hatch philosophy dictates that you match the size, shape, and color of the natural.

A good match typically results in an imitation that looks somewhat like the natural.

blood, which it cannot resist, or the trude-style wing is a dead giveaway for a caddisfly or stonefly. The hocus-pocus guys will say that if the trude wing is tied in a precise tent configuration it concentrates universal forces in the same way that a pyramid does and . . . well maybe we just don't know exactly what makes a good attractor pattern work. I'm just happy it does. And you can double that joy because I can't explain why.

Most of the fly fishers I know are match-the-hatch devotees. The basics of matching the hatch are easy. You make observations of what the trout are eating and then match that natural's size, color, and silhouette as closely as possible with an artificial fly. You apply the rules equally to immature and mature life stages of aquatic insects and other trout foods. How far beyond the basics you go is up to you.

The match-the-hatch philosophy has served me well over the decades. I think I've caught more trout and learned more about the world the trout live in because of it. Nothing beats having a rational system for explaining why a fly worked in a particular situation. It keeps you going when times are tough and gives you hope that somewhere down the road in a similar situation you should be able to repeat your success. But it pays to remember that it is just a system. The other side of the coin is the attractor fly. For a while in the 1970s if you even brought up attractor fishing, other anglers looked at you like you'd gone over to the dark side. It was like cheating on your sweetheart. How could you even think about going out on the river; tying on a big, bushy, high-floating dry fly that didn't imitate anything in the real world; and then casting it willy-nilly all over the place? It was just too damn carefree. Needless to say I had to try it. I knew all those attractor-fly fishers up in Montana were smiling about something.

Anyway, time passes. Fly fishers change. The pendulum swings, and attractor fly patterns seem to be coming into vogue once again. I like fishing attractor dry flies because it is so carefree. It's the freewheeling, elemental simplicity that draws me. Typically, the flies are big enough to see, and you get to make lots of casts with a single, unweighted fly that often elicits explosive and exciting strikes.

But is it possible that, as freewheeling as the idea of attractors is, we are somehow restricting ourselves? It all comes down to how you define attractor. Does an attractor pattern necessarily have to be large? I fish size 18 Griffith's Gnats up against the banks a lot when there's nothing going on. It's a fly that can imitate a beetle or a midge cluster or some kind of emerging whatchamacallit. The palmered hackle is just plain fishy on any pattern. It holds the fly up off the water on a hundred points of hackle tip. It creates the illusion of life. Whether you call that an element of attraction or not, it catches the trout's attention for sure.

How about downsizing the Royal Coachman? My friend Roger Hill, who is one of the best fly fishers I know, once revealed to me that a size 18 or 20 Coachman is one of his go-to flies when the midge hatch comes off on the Arkansas River. If you think about it, almost any fly pattern can be fished as an attractor. I do it with tiny Adams parachutes

Is it possible for a match-the-hatch pattern to serve as an attractor pattern in some cases?

all the time. My size 20 CDC Blue-Winged Olive imitation is a killer searcher fly on slower moving water, especially if I drag, scoot, or twitch it just a little!

It's all about definitions, but in fishing, a definition is sometimes nothing other than a mindset. I think that if we broaden our definitions of attractor pattern fishing, we'll find that we can actually fish match-the-hatch imitations like we would a traditional attractor fly when there isn't a hatch, or fish smaller versions of traditional attractor patterns in match-the-hatch situations. It may be more productive to think about fishing attractors in four broad categories that may, depending on the situation, overlap.

1. It's often useful to actively fish attractor fly patterns.
2. Attractor fly pattern design should focus primarily on the water type where you plan to fish the fly.
3. An attractor pattern can be successfully fished during a hatch and, conversely, a match-the-hatch pattern can be successfully fished as an attractor when no insects are hatching.
4. Subsurface fly patterns can be attractors.

You may be thinking that this is beginning to sound a lot less freewheeling than you want your attractor fishing to be, but it's really only an attempt at bending a few fly-fishing mindsets. And the first one that comes to mind is the cult of the drag-free drift. There's no doubt that some situations require that the fly drift with as little drag as possible. Many of those situations occur during a hatch. But sometimes the rules change when there isn't a hatch. And then there's the idea that matching the hatch should be the basis of all fly-fishing thought. There's no doubt that matching the hatch is probably the most satisfying and productive strategy for catching a trout on a fly, but it's not the only way. And besides, you may just find that your match-the-hatch and drag-free drift philosophy hasn't been quite as pure as you thought. It may be you've been unknowingly applying some attractor strategies all along. There's nothing wrong with that either. You may even want to consciously apply a few of them to your drag-free, match-the-hatch game when the trout aren't buying it.

With this in mind, let's take a look at the techniques and fly pattern types you'll need to become a more complete attractor fly fisherman.

FISHING THE ACTIVE FLY

To some degree, attractor fly fishing has always emphasized the active fly. In *The Dry Fly and Fast Water*, a groundbreaking book published in 1914, George LaBranche addressed catching trout in faster moving water where no rising fish were observed. One technique he described was how to actively bounce a dry-fly imitation on faster water to elicit a strike. But he also emphasized how a high-riding dry fly could be successfully fished with traditional drag-free-drift tactics through fast water too. He even goes as far as saying that a dry-fly pattern doesn't necessarily have to match a natural.

This kind of thinking laid the groundwork for a system of fishing dry flies when the trout weren't rising where you use traditional drag-free drifts to systematically search water that doesn't have any defining surface features. In the most basic application you initially make a fan pattern of searching casts close to yourself, and then extend the length of the casts another few feet out and so on until you cover all the water. When surface features are present, make casts to spots where trout are likely to lie, such as in front of and behind rocks, tails of pools, near banks, where currents of fast and slow water merge, and where the water enters a pool. If flies fished on the dead drift don't elicit a strike, then impart action to the fly by allowing it to skitter, swing, or drag at the end of the drift.

Although drag-free presentations are still a very important part of my attractor fishing game, especially in slower-moving water, more and more I find myself activating the fly at some stage of the drift. Most often it's nothing more than a subtle twitch or two just to make the fly stand out and possibly arouse the curiosity of a trout. If a twitch, swing, or skitter does work, the reward is almost always a crashing strike.

Here are some ideas for fishing a more active dry fly. Keep in mind that fishing an active dry fly requires an active fisherman. Remember that you are searching water—you want to cover as many likely (and unlikely) places where a trout might be holding, but don't belabor the point. The odds are if a trout is going to strike an active fly, it will be on the first or second presentation. If you don't get a response, move on.

Splash & Crash

This maneuver works best within four or five feet of grassy banks or around sweepers (trees that have fallen into the river). The classic fly to use is a grasshopper, but I've had equal success with Trude-style patterns. The most important thing to remember

The object of the splash & crash is to splat the fly on the water's surface. PHOTO BY KYLE HENDRICKS

here is to forget everything you ever learned about presentation. The object is to land the fly on the water's surface with a bit of a splat. In this case, the commotion is a good thing. The idea is that the mother-of-all-trout will be loafing around near the bank, sense the disturbance, and wheel instinctively to eat the hopper or whatever it is that's been unfortunate enough to hit the water so close by. Expect heartstopping, crashing strikes . . . and sometimes a surprisingly large trout.

It is possible in some situations to overdo the crash. Sometimes a larger attractor-style fly makes enough commotion on the water's surface if it's just cast in a normal manner. This is particularly true in calmer waters and if you are casting to a non-feeding trout that you have spotted. Actually, there is a nice variation of the splash & crash that you might want to employ on those non-feeding trout that you do see. Try to softly land the attractor fly just behind the trout's eye and a foot or so away from it. Sometimes the fish will instinctively turn and hammer it.

The time to dial up the crash part of this presentation is when you're fishing heavier water or the wind is up.

Plop & Drop

The only similarity between the in-your-face splash & crash and the delicate plop & drop is that they both work best near the bank. For the plop & drop, cast the fly up on the grassy bank and then pull it into the water. This takes a bit more casting finesse than you might think. The object is to make a soft delivery so the fly doesn't get caught in the grass and can then be gently pulled into the water. If you're having trouble making that soft delivery, try underpowering the forward casting stroke a bit to soften the fly's landing.

The trout will often strike the moment the fly drops onto the water and is still drag free or at the moment the current begins to drag the fly. The drag-free strike may be a subtle sip or kiss. When the fly begins to drag, expect the strike to be more explosive. I like Elk Hair Caddisflies, Greased Muddlers, Trudes, and Antron-Wing Spent Spinners for the plop & drop, but my all-time favorite plop & drop fly is a grasshopper pattern.

  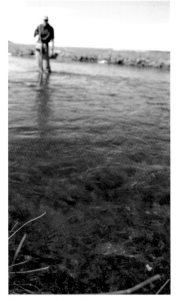

Left: Use a soft delivery to cast the fly into the grass along the bank. *Middle:* Gently pull the fly from the grass into the water close to the bank. Many strikes occur right when the fly hits the water. *Right:* Continue the drift. A strike may occur when the fly begins to drag in the current.

Slap & Dap

Use the slap & dap in pocketwater and wherever you find rocks in the flow. The idea is to bounce the fly off a rock after which it typically falls straight down to the water below. If done properly, the fly will fall in the soft cushion of water within a few inches of rock, and left over slack from the cast will allow it to sit there for a moment. That's plenty of time for the trout that are taking advantage of that cushion to strike the fly.

One thing to be careful about with the slap & dap is to not hit the rock too hard with the fly. If you do, you could break the

Bounce a dry fly off the rock by slightly underpowering the cast.
PHOTO BY KYLE HENDRICKS

The fly will land in the cushion of water next to the rock where trout often hold. The underpowered cast will pile up enough leader to allow a drag-free drift.
PHOTO BY KYLE HENDRICKS

Continue the drift along the rock. Check the fly hook occasionally to make sure it didn't fracture when it hit the rock.
PHOTO BY KYLE HENDRICKS

hook point. You should periodically check the hook whenever you employ the slap & dap just to be sure it hasn't been broken. I like more fully hackled flies like the Renegade and palmer-hackled attractors for the slap & dap because the hackle protects the hook point.

Drag & Nag

After I've made a standard across-and-upstream or down-and-across drag-free presentation with an attractor dry fly, I sometimes allow it to skate, scoot, and drag against the current at the end of the drift. It's another case of forgetting all those niceties of the traditional dry-fly man's world. A properly executed drag & nag should cause the fly to make a slight to moderate V wake in the water. Too much drag and disturbance will often put the trout down. As the fly is motorboating across the current, I like to nag it with some twitches from the rod tip that cause the fly to hop or skip over the surface.

I use bushy, palmer-hackled flies for the drag & nag because they make more commotion on the water's surface and don't tend to dive like some Trude patterns or traditionally hackled patterns do.

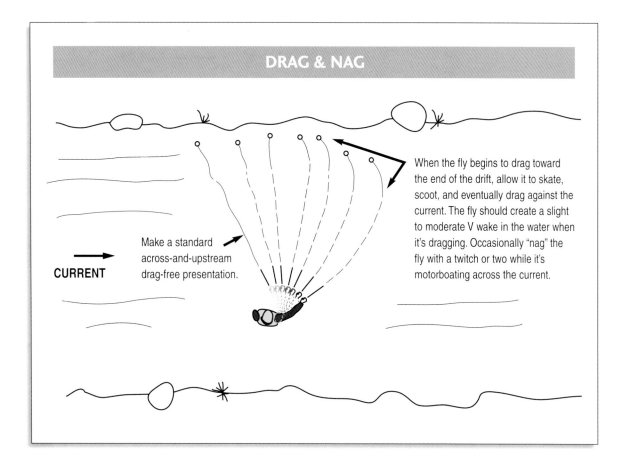

DRAG & NAG

CURRENT

Make a standard across-and-upstream drag-free presentation.

When the fly begins to drag toward the end of the drift, allow it to skate, scoot, and eventually drag against the current. The fly should create a slight to moderate V wake in the water when it's dragging. Occasionally "nag" the fly with a twitch or two while it's motorboating across the current.

THE SUDDEN INCH

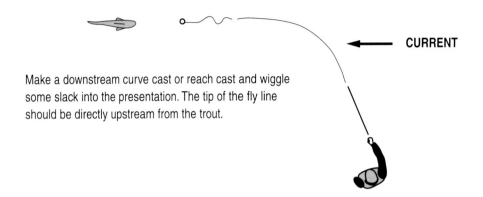

Make a downstream curve cast or reach cast and wiggle some slack into the presentation. The tip of the fly line should be directly upstream from the trout.

CURRENT

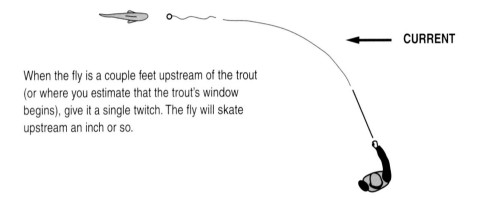

When the fly is a couple feet upstream of the trout (or where you estimate that the trout's window begins), give it a single twitch. The fly will skate upstream an inch or so.

CURRENT

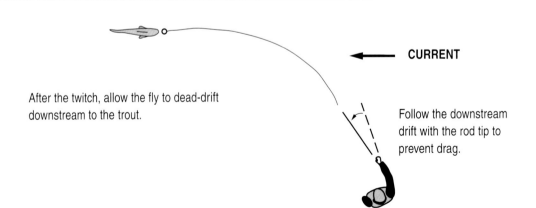

After the twitch, allow the fly to dead-drift downstream to the trout.

CURRENT

Follow the downstream drift with the rod tip to prevent drag.

Sudden Inch

The sudden inch is a drag & nag presentation with class. Leonard M. Wright Jr. introduced the sudden inch in his 1972 book *Fishing the Dry Fly as a Living Insect.* Since that time his unorthodox method has spawned a number of active dry-fly tactics. The object of the sudden inch is to twitch an attractor dry fly upstream in a series of short jerks. To accomplish this, make a downstream curve cast or a reach cast. Either cast, when properly executed, will put your fly directly downstream of the line and leader. If you lift the rod just a little, the fly will jerk upstream a bit, and then if you immediately drop the rod tip, the fly will float drag-free downstream for an inch or two. You've just performed a sudden inch and in the process made a darn good imitation of an egg-laying caddisfly making its way upstream.

Needless to say, the Elk Caddis is an ideal fly pattern for this tactic. Other palmer-hackled patterns work well too. You should avoid traditionally hackled fly designs because they tend to dive under the surface rather than skate. In a pinch, trim the bottom half of the hackle to get the fly to skate.

Down & Dirty

The final active fly tactic is probably the easiest of all. Simply pull the fly under the water at any point in the drift. To execute the down & dirty, tighten up on the line and pull the dry fly under with either the fly line itself or the rod tip. Actually, fly fishers often inadvertently pull a fly under at the end of a drag-free drift and are pleasantly surprised when they get a strike! Well, you can pull the dry fly under any time you want and get strikes. The buoyant nature of a dry fly pulled under the surface can be quite alluring to trout.

FLY PATTERNS FOR WATER TYPES

When you say attractor fly, most fishermen think of large, high-riding, big-profile fly patterns such as Wulffs, Humpies, or Stimulators that vaguely look like something, but more important, won't get waterlogged too quickly when fished in the fast water or swung across the current. Other patterns used as attractors imitate a terrestrial, such as a grasshopper, beetle, or ant; such insects typically aren't available to the trout in huge numbers, but are available sporadically throughout much of the season and may elicit a strike even though a natural hasn't been encountered on the water for weeks or even months.

Some fishermen point out that a hopper pattern isn't really an attractor pattern because it actually imitates an insect. That's true, too, but I can go either way because a

A dancing fly, like the Bivisible, is designed to skitter and dance over the water's surface on stiff hackle points.

Most fly fishers think of attractor flies as large, high-riding, big-profile patterns.

hopper or ant or beetle will work in such a broad range of situations that it may in fact be a match-the-hatch imitation in one locale and an attractor pattern in another. Other fly fishers define an attractor pattern as a fly that incorporates a broadly based characteristic that the trout will mistake as food. These same fly fishers often assign the name "searcher pattern" to another category of flies that don't resemble food in any way but provoke a trout's curiosity or interest to the point that it strikes the fly. Although these are interesting and possibly useful distinctions, I've always referred to all of these fly types simply as attractors. I base my definition more on how I fish the fly than why a trout takes the fly.

Anyway, for most fly fishers the high-riding, big-profile kind of flies and terrestrials are the extent of the pattern types that they experiment with in typical dry-fly attractor-fishing situations, although a few

older anglers might occasionally fish what I call dancing-fly pattern types. These are lightly dressed flies that stand up tall on stiff hackle points and skitter and dance over the water's surface. The Bivisible is the classic example. In many cases, all that is required is hackle and a thread body. Any palmer-hackled fly also fits the bill. And, of course, there is Hewitt's mostly forgotten skating spider that requires the use of very stiff oversized hackle on a small, short-shank hook (see chapter 8).

Fly fishers who are new to attractor fishing almost always fish whatever pattern style they choose without much regard to the water type. The reasoning seems to be that if it's an attractor fly, it should attract a strike any way you cast it. Most anglers realize pretty quickly, though, that this is not the case. You find out, for example, that the high-rider fly you most favor seems to be most productive in a certain water type. Let's

Scott Sanchez's Convertible meets all the criteria for a heavy water fly when left in its bulky, untrimmed version.

The Convertible has a broad silhouette as seen from the trout's point of view, which makes it more visible in heavier water.

say that water type is typically a riffle of moderate depth moving at a moderate speed. Once you make that important connection, it doesn't take long before you find yourself seeking out that particular water type where your fly pattern is most successful, while either totally ignoring or underfishing other water types that might also be fertile ground for attractor fishing.

The paradox, of course, is that a basic tenet of attractor-style fishing is to cover all the fishable water, but you happen to know that you get most of your strikes when you match the water type to the fly. It makes a kind of quirky, reverse match-the-hatch sense. So what do you do about the rest of the water where the fly isn't productive? Well, nobody said that just because you're fishing an attractor fly you have to cover all the water with just one fly pattern style!

The point is that if you want to move to the next level of attractor fishing, you will need to consider matching the fly pattern style to the water type you're fishing. That means when you fish a heavy riffle or rough water, you want a buoyant, larger-size fly that gives a broad silhouette from the trout's viewpoint. The trout's ability to see a fly in heavier water types is limited, and a pattern style with these characteristics is most likely to catch a trout's attention. Flies with hair wings tied in Trude style and long bodies that sit down on the water's surface fit the bill. Other enhancements might include a deer-hair bullet head to bulk up the silhouette and rubber legs for added action. Hackle is okay on these broad silhouette patterns if you either tie it or cut it to hook-gap length or shorter. Long, stiff hackle lifts even a large fly from the surface, making it more difficult for the trout to see in rough water.

Fly patterns along the lines of Scott Sanchez's Convertible come to mind for fishing heavier water. Sanchez designed the fly for the Jackson Hole One-Fly competition. He based it on existing proven patterns that could be trimmed down to meet changing conditions on the river. Sanchez called his creation a Wooly Bugger/Tarantula/ Trude/Wulff. The fly could be trimmed to create a mayfly profile, imitate various emergers, or pass as a streamer or even a nymph. If the fly is left in its bulkier untrimmed form, it meets all of the criteria for fishing heavier riffles or rough water. It's

A large spent spinner imitation with clear Antron wings is a good attractor pattern for slower moving water.

buoyant, sits low on the water, has a broad silhouette from the trout's viewpoint, and is easy for the angler to see.

More moderate water flows require a fly with a different profile. That's where a longer, stiff, dry-fly hackle may help the fly drift a bit faster and more erratically, which will force the trout to attack it quickly. The more traditional attractor patterns such as Wulffs and the Royal Coachman with upright wings seem to work best in these water types. This is also the water type to use your high-riding lightweight attractors such as the Bivisible. The Bivisible is a fly that begs to be fished in an active way. Once in a while I cast it across and upstream and give it a few twitches during the drift, but most of the time I cast it across and downstream and twitch, skitter, or hop it over the surface.

Ultimately you'll have to decide which pattern styles best fit the basic water types on your home water. You could end up with two or three different flies that pretty much cover you for heavy to moderate water types or decide on a single pattern like Sanchez's Convertible that you can trim to meet your needs.

Slow water types have always baffled fly fishers when it comes to attractors. It's pretty obvious that plopping a size 12 Stimmy down on glassy water probably won't turn the trick. Your first instinct is almost always to go to a downsized, standard, attractor-style pattern or even switch over to a terrestrial. And these are, in fact, all steps in the right direction, especially if you concentrate your casts toward shady areas, banks, and any subtle seams or current aberrations that you see.

A less obvious pattern type for slow-moving water is the spent mayfly spinner. I

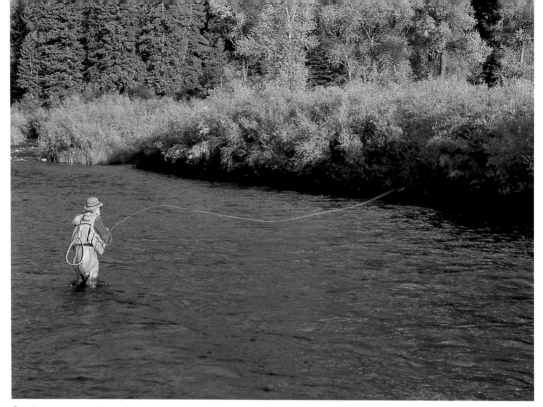

Casting a spent spinner imitation up against the banks when nothing is happening can be an effective attractor fishing technique.

learned this a number of years ago when I was marking time on a meadow stretch of my favorite Rocky Mountain tailwater. There was no hatch, but I wasn't ready to rig up for nymphing yet. It was the kind of lazy water where every once in a while I'd see a rise come out of nowhere. Most fly fishers show a passing interest in random rises and then revert to scanning the surface in hopes of finding a trout feeding in a more predictable pattern that they can match a fly imitation to. I would have done the same when I observed another stray rise, but I just happened to notice a single nondescript spent mayfly spinner floating on the water's surface at about the same time. My first thought was that it's a bit unusual to see a spent spinner on the surface when there's nothing else going on. But then it occurred to me that

everything doesn't always fit neatly under the bell curve. There's bound to be a few mayflies here and there that emerge before or after the main hatch, or they might simply be leftovers. The spent mayfly spinner I observed could actually have been a dun, live spinner, or cripple that had somehow ended up on the surface in a spent position.

One thing led to another and I rummaged through my fly boxes until I found a size 14 Rusty Spinner imitation. It's a little big for here, I thought, but what the heck. I'll at least get a little casting practice in. I started off by just casting the fly helterskelter over the flat water. The first indication that I might be on to something was a swirl that appeared near the fly.

I then decided to concentrate my efforts on the undercut bank on the opposite side

Try casting a spent spinner imitation into eddies and backwaters where the naturals may be concentrated long after the spinnerfall.

of the stream, figuring that a trout might be lurking in the shadows. I made presentations within a foot of the bank and sometimes even cast up onto the bank and pulled the spinner imitation into the flow the same way I'd do with a grasshopper or beetle imitation. When I cast the fly behind a little tuft of grass that protruded out into the flow, its drift was ended by a gentle sip. Ten minutes later, I released a 17-inch brown trout. And I became a believer in the spent spinner as an attractor fly pattern.

Up until that day, like most dry-fly fishers, I'd always reserved my spent spinner imitations for when I found trout rising to spent mayflies on the water's surface. The closest I ever got to fishing the spent spinner as an attractor was a few occasions when I used it to see if any fish might still be interested an hour or two after the trout had gone off a

spent spinnerfall. It had never occurred to me that during dry-fly season there's probably always a few spent mayflies on the surface for one reason or another. And even if there aren't, the trout would surely recognize one, and being the opportunists that they are they might snatch an imitation out of the drift if it were properly presented. A proper presentation would, like any proper spent spinner presentation whether there's a spinnerfall or not, have to be drag free.

Over the years, I've developed a system for fishing spent spinner imitations when there are no naturals on the surface. None of these tactics are new or revolutionary—you have probably used them fishing other pattern types at other times—but the trick is to apply those ideas to fishing spent spinner imitations in a new way.

I have two basic strategies for fishing spent spinner patterns as attractors. If I know that spinnerfalls of a specific species have recently occurred, I fish an imitation of that species even when no naturals are on the surface. If there hasn't been any recent spinnerfalls, I fish large size 14 to size 10 imitations. The larger spinner patterns act as slow-water attractor patterns and are easy to see on the water's surface. I tie them with thinly dubbed bodies of black, rusty brown, olive, and dirty yellow or white. Although I've experimented with a number of materials for the wings over the years, I've found clear Antron to be the most effective if only because it's easier to see on the water's surface.

The tactics for fishing a spent spinner as an attractor differ in several ways from how you'd fish the pattern during an actual spinnerfall. The slowly moving water within a foot or two of the bank is the most consistently productive, but it never hurts to put the fly anywhere you think a trout might be holding or over a fish that you've spotted. The presentation has to be drag free, so make sure your reach cast, parachute cast, and other slack-producing casts are up to snuff and accurate.

The critical point to remember is that your first few casts are probably your most important casts. That means that unlike fishing an actual spinnerfall where you can stay in one place and make many casts to trout that are working the naturals, it pays to cover a lot of water when fishing spent spinners as attractors. I move upstream while casting against the opposite bank and to any other water that looks productive. Give each likely looking spot a pop or two and then move on to the next. Remember, you are searching for trout that are looking up for the opportunity to take whatever drifts by or whatever piques their curiosity.

The one exception to the cast-and-move strategy is if you get a swirl or slash to the fly, but the trout misses it. That deserves a few more well-cast drag-free presentations. If you find that you are consistently getting swirls but no hookups, try changing to a smaller imitation and double-check to be sure there is no drag in the presentation.

Although I usually use imitations of spent mayfly spinners, I should mention that I'm occasionally successful with a greased Hare's Ear Soft Hackle or similar soft hackle pattern fished as an attractor on top. I reason that these imitations may represent a spent caddisfly or crippled mayfly dun that's left over from a hatch or for some other reason has ended up on the surface. The downside to these patterns used as attractors is that they are more difficult to see on the water, but nonetheless, they are worth a shot if the spent spinner isn't producing.

A final general consideration for all your attractor patterns is color. Fly fishers can spend hours discussing color when it comes to fly patterns, and I'll be the first to admit that I'm not as obsessive as most. I do try to match the color of naturals when matching the hatch, but I believe that fly size and shape are often more important than color. Surprisingly, I'm a bit more of a colorist when it comes to attractor fly patterns because I think the right color can make the fly more visible to trout and that's a big part of what attraction is all about.

Having said that, though, I can't really say that I've made anything close to a scientific study of what colors should be most attractive to trout and why. Everything I believe in I've learned by simply trying different color flies on the water. That experience over the years has led me to a preference for the colors red, yellow, orange, chartreuse (or lime), or black for the main body of an attractor dry fly. As a rule, I use just one of my preferred colors for the body and, if possible, try to include peacock herl somewhere on the fly. When it comes to hair wings (either upright or Trude style) I like white the best, although bleached elk or deer hair is a close second. For more lightly dressed dancing fly attractor patterns, I still prefer the above colors for the body assuming I tie a body at all, but I don't think they are as important as the action of the fly over the water's surface.

ATTRACTOR FLIES FOR HATCHES & MATCH-THE-HATCH FLIES AS ATTRACTORS

A number of years ago, Mike Lawson, the renowned Henry's Fork guide, and others began to popularize the idea of unmatching the hatch. They had found that, during very heavy hatches or spinnerfalls, it was sometimes best to fish a fly that *didn't* imitate the naturals on the water. The logic was that it might be better to have a fly that stood out from the hundreds or even thousands of insects on the water. Lawson ultimately settled on unmatching many hatches with a beetle imitation because it clearly didn't match the hatch but the trout were familiar with beetles because they saw them sporadically over the course of the season. The same logic held true for using an ant pattern. Other anglers preferred downsized versions of classic attractor-style flies such as a size 18 Royal Wulff. All of these strategies proved

themselves on the selective trout of the Henry's Fork and other spring creeks and tailwaters throughout the Rocky Mountains. In more extreme cases of frustration, even larger sized attractor fly patterns sometimes got the trout's attention. The point was if your match-the-hatch imitations weren't working, why not show the trout something totally different? And that is a good point to remember.

You might also want to note that you can extend this idea of fishing attractors beyond the realm of heavily feeding tailwater or spring creek trout. A little Royal Wulff or spent spinner imitation might just save your bacon when you can't find the combination to unlock the mysteries of a pod of trout rising to midges on your favorite freestone in the dead of the winter. And the powers of terrestrials fished as attractors anytime and anywhere are well known.

Another consideration is the use of what might be termed crossover match-the-hatch/attractor dry-fly patterns as pure attractors. Fly fishers often associate such favorites as the Adams, Elk Hair Caddis, Griffith's Gnat, or Comparadun more with match-the-hatch-type tactics, but find themselves either knowingly or unwittingly fishing them as attractors during hatches. An example is the fly fisher who settles on the Adams during a caddisfly hatch even though he knows it doesn't imitate the natural that closely, but he is confident in its ability to produce trout under most circumstances. The obvious next step here is to fish these patterns as attractors when there is no hatch at all.

This same logic extends beyond these match-the-hatch crossover patterns. I have

Downsizing a classic attractor pattern may be the answer when all match-the-hatch efforts fail.

A match-the-hatch fly pattern such as this CDC Blue-Winged Olive Comparadun imitation can be used to successfully search the water when nothing is hatching.

had great days searching the water with tiny size 20 CDC Blue-Winged Olive imitations. Most trout are familiar with a mayfly, and if they're in the mood and you pass a pretty good imitation of a mayfly over them, the odds are pretty good they'll eat it.

You can fine-tune your match-the-hatch pattern fished as an attractor by broadly matching the imitations to water type. It doesn't make a lot of sense to run a delicate size 18 CDC mayfly dun imitation through heavy water (although I've done it and had a few surprises), but you might do well fishing it along the edges of the heavy water or in water types where you'd expect to find mayflies hatching. I've had good success along the edges where riffles run out into pools, up along banks, and where the water is moving fast enough that the trout must quickly decide whether to strike or not.

SUBSURFACE ATTRACTOR PATTERNS

It's not hard to make the argument that all nymph patterns are imitations rather than attractors. You can solidify that argument even further by stating all nymph patterns that you fish with dead-drift nymphing techniques are imitations because you are actually imitating the behavior of the naturals when you dead-drift them. I've heard the argument often and I sort of agree with it, but I can also say that there are a number of nymph patterns—such as the Gold-Ribbed Hare's Ear, Pheasant Tail, Brassie, San Juan Worm, and Prince Nymph—that seem more attractive to trout over a broader range of conditions than a lot of other nymph patterns. You can enhance this attractiveness even more by adding a little flashy pearlescent Mylar or Krystal Flash.

So maybe whether these patterns are attractors is just a matter of semantics. I can tell you that if you decide to consider them attractors, you'll probably fish them more often and in a greater variety of conditions and I think you'll catch trout most everywhere you go. It may not be as many trout as another nympher who's got the naturals dialed in and matched them, but you'll catch trout. I like to toss out the challenge that if you give me a Gold-Ribbed Hare's Ear, Prince Nymph, and Pheasant Tail in the right size (larger for freestone streams, smaller for spring creeks and tailwaters), I can catch a trout anywhere.

When you broaden the scope of subsurface flies to include wet flies, lifted flies, or streamers, everything changes because these flies are being activated by the angler; as we noted earlier, an active fly is almost always an attractor fly. Once we agree that these patterns can indeed be attractors, then it makes sense that adding a little flash to a streamer might not hurt and that color might also be important. I almost always believe in using some flash on a subsurface fly, and when it comes to color, the ones that seem the most attractive to trout on the surface also seem to work well below the surface. But there are always exceptions when it comes to a fly's color. The color blue immediately comes to mind as a leading exception . . . but we'll talk more about that when we talk about small fly triggers (see chapter 8).

It took me a long time to warm to the idea of fishing attractors. More than anything I think I needed the confidence of nine or ten fly boxes in my vest that I thought held a fly to match every phase of every hatch I might encounter on my home water. It's the classic silver bullet approach: you think there is a fly-pattern solution to every fly-fishing problem. It's nothing more than an extreme version of the match-the-hatch philosophy, and for the most part I'm still a match-the-hatch fisherman. But it's a big world out there, and there's something to be said for the freedom of a day spent where you change your dry-fly pattern once or twice or maybe not at all and just cover a lot of water to see what happens.

CHAPTER 3

Tight-Line Tactics

Experimenting with presentations for streamers, wet flies, emergers, and dry flies

It's been a good many years since A. K. Best and I fished the autumn Blue-Winged Olive spinnerfall on the South Platte River. We were regulars there before the catastrophic Hayman wildfire in 2002 changed that river and the surrounding country for what will surely be the rest of my life and probably many years thereafter. We had one of those unspoken agreements that fishermen make to always try to meet up on a river at the same time each year because, at least in our case, the spinnerfall had been some of the most challenging fly fishing either of us had ever been witness to. To begin with, you could figure that by October the olive spinners would be an honest size 24, which was considerably smaller than the size 20s in the spring. In addition, the natural wasn't very olive at all. Most of the spinners had a brown body with at best a hint of olive. But they were indeed olives because I had taken a specimen to the Colorado College biology lab and meticulously keyed it to the *Baetis* genus with a powerful stereo microscope.

The funny thing was that we never found out when the duns were hatching, but anytime from about noon on you could expect to see the spinners over the absolutely crystalline water. It's impossible to describe the light on the water and the crispness of the air at that time of year. So we would wait around hoping the spinners would fall and be followed by the subtle dimpling of feeding trout. It was the most technical fly fishing that either A. K. or I had ever done, and we celebrated every trout that we hooked up. It was a sweet business, and every time we met on the river we'd each have a few new fly patterns that we'd tied with the knowledge we'd gained on the previous trip.

But like all great fishing, there were occasional glitches such as the day the spinners didn't come off at all. That might not sound like a big deal, but remember it's late fall on a tailwater. The flows are on the low side and the water is crystal clear. And it is surprisingly difficult to catch or even see a trout without the spinners. But that was the case one afternoon when we were standing by a nice riffle run scratching our heads trying to figure out what to do. That's when A. K. laughed and said, "When in doubt or when all is lost fish a Woolly." He then proceeded to cut back his leader to about a 4X. While he was shuffling through his fly boxes, he talked about how a Woolly Bugger was always good for a fish when he had lived in Michigan and he'd found the same to be true in times of need in the Rockies. Of course, I teased him because I'd really only ever seen him fish a dry fly.

Before long he had a black and olive Woolly Bugger tied on to what was now a 7-foot leader and was casting it across and slightly downstream. He then allowed it to swing across the riffle. Sometimes he threw a mend in to get down, but most of the time he controlled the speed and depth that the fly would swing by how much he cast it downstream—the greater the downstream angle, the faster and more shallow the fly traveled. It couldn't have been ten minutes before a wake came up behind the fly and A. K.'s unmistakable fish-on laugh rang out up and down the river. In a few minutes he released a nice 14-inch brown trout. "So there you have it. All is not lost," he said.

That was my entry into what I called the uncommon world of streamers, because to my way of thinking A. K. fished that fly under very unusual streamer conditions. It was autumn, the water was low and crystal clear, and the sun was bright. I thought you fished streamers in the spring when the water was up and maybe off-color or at least when there was a better flow. But the fish-on laugh was unmistakable and impossible to counterfeit. It meant, as always, that A. K. was on to something.

I kept thinking about out-of-the-box streamer fishing until the next spring when I came up with an off-the-wall, but possibly educational, idea. Well, at least it sounded interesting to me, but I got the sense my pals thought it was a bit idiotic. I had discovered Dan Byford's Zonker streamer pattern a few years before. It was the newest fly pattern craze at the time, and I'd tied a few and done well in lakes. I hadn't fished them seriously in rivers yet, but the few times that I did I managed to catch fish or at least miss some strikes.

My foolish plan was that I would fish the Cheesman Canyon section of the South Platte for the entire summer with just a Zonker pattern. This might not sound like such a big deal if you're from Wyoming, Michigan, or other streamer country, but the South Platte was the center of the world for technical dry-fly and nymph fishing with very small flies. A. K. was probably one of the few fishermen who went to the river with any streamers in his box at all, and he only had two or three Woolly Buggers. The rest of us pretty much had flies that were size 18 or smaller.

I'd never tried fishing a streamer in the canyon even when the flows were high. But, I figured, what did I have to lose? If worse came to worse, I'd just admit to my buddies that I was a weirdo, which they already knew, and go back to fishing the small stuff. So it began. I went into the canyon with a single fly box of weighted and unweighted size 4 and size 6 Zonkers and a 6-weight graphite rod with a 7-foot leader tapered to 2X.

Although my friend Dana Tellin had taught me a few streamer tricks on the Arkansas River when I lived in Salida, Colorado, I was for all practical purposes starting from scratch. That meant I fished the basic across-and-downstream presentation pretty much the way all the fly-fishing magazines said to do it. With practice, I learned to control the speed and the depth of the swing. And as amateurish as my beginnings were, I can say that my stream log noted two rainbow trout caught on the first day. They weren't the monsters that the fly-fishing magazines always imply you should catch with streamers, but they were respectable fish for a neophyte tight liner.

I didn't give up on it for the better part of three months and fished Zonkers well into September. There were a few periods of moderately high flows, but most of the time the river was running at its summer normal, which for the South Platte is pretty thin. I learned to make short swings in tight water, use unweighted Zonkers on longer leaders in slow or shallow water, fish to structure, and even high-stick weighted streamers on a barely tight line in hard-to-reach places. I fished upstream, downstream, across stream, and in between. And to my surprise, I almost always caught a trout or two, and many of them came from water two feet deep or less. I have no doubt that I would have caught more trout fishing a tiny nymph on the dead drift, but I was truly surprised by the number of trout I managed to fool under a range of weather and water conditions on Colorado's

A Zonker streamer consistently produced trout from what is considered highly technical small-fly water.

premier technical small-fly river. I can also say that I was surprised by the number of average-size trout that nailed the Zonker. I did catch some very nice-size specimens too, but once again I think I could have done better on the big boys fishing nymphs on a short line.

So you're probably wondering what the point is if I could catch more and larger trout by using the accepted small-fly tactics for this water. On a more esoteric level, I would say that I liked the idea that as a fly fisherman I could choose *how* I wanted to catch a fish and that it didn't have to be about size and numbers every time I was on the water. Needless to say, when you're trying to catch fish the way you want, you may not catch anything when your pals are—but then again when you do land one it is sweet indeed.

On a more practical level, which is the level I tend to pay the most attention to, I've found that my little forays to the edge of what is commonly accepted fly-fishing wisdom have at times opened whole new areas of the sport that I never considered. In this case, I learned the power of fishing the tight line, which in my area was not a commonly practiced tactic. And in the process and over the years, it's opened my eyes up to a variety of ways that flies of all types can be fished on a tight line. And that was something to learn because at that time on the South Platte River the drag-free drift was king.

I know better now, and surprisingly I see more and more anglers on the South Platte and other technical waters experimenting with tight-line presentations of streamers, wet flies, emergers, and even dry flies.

That's why I wasn't too surprised recently when I learned about a new secret technique that South Platte River guides were using for beginning fly fishers who are having trouble mastering short-line, dead-drift nymphing tactics.

First, the guide takes off the strike indicator and any weight attached to the leader.

Guides find that a soft-hackle wet-fly pattern fished on the swing helps their clients who are having a difficult time mastering dead-drift nymphing techniques.

He then removes the small fly and ties on a size 14 soft-hackle wet fly. He instructs the client to cast across and downstream as best he can and to let the floating line swing with the current. When the fly finishes the swing and is directly downstream, it's time to strip it back upstream and cast again. The guide stresses that as long as the current swings the fly, the cast doesn't have to be perfect. Surprisingly, the clients hook up with amazing consistency.

Well-versed fly fishers will recognize this "secret" technique as nothing more than a classic wet-fly, or tight-line, presentation. Until the late 1960s, it was probably the most popular technique for fishing a subsurface fly. Today, fly fishers still employ basic across-and-downstream tight-line tactics when they fish streamers and the close-to-forgotten wet flies, but the true art and versatility of the tight-line presentation has largely fallen into disuse.

That's a shame because even a basic facility with a tight line opens up all kinds of fly-fishing possibilities, and if you're willing to entertain a broader definition of tight lining that includes dry flies and emerging nymphs or pupae, a whole new realm of fly-fishing options opens up. The best place to begin is with a review of basic tight-line techniques that includes some new ways to look at how to control the speed and depth of the fly, which in many cases may be more important than the fly pattern itself.

SUBSURFACE TIGHT-LINE TECHNIQUE

A subsurface tight-line presentation uses the current to move a fly in a way that entices a trout to strike. Theories as to *why* a trout strikes a swung fly differ: the fly may imitate

BASIC QUARTERING ACROSS-AND-DOWNSTREAM TIGHT-LINE PRESENTATION

Cast the fly quartering across and downstream. The current drags the fly line, causing the fly to swing across the river. PHOTO BY JANA RUSH

When the line straightens at the end of the swing, strip the fly back upstream to your position.
PHOTO BY JANA RUSH

CAST ANGLE, SWING ARC, AND FLY SPEED

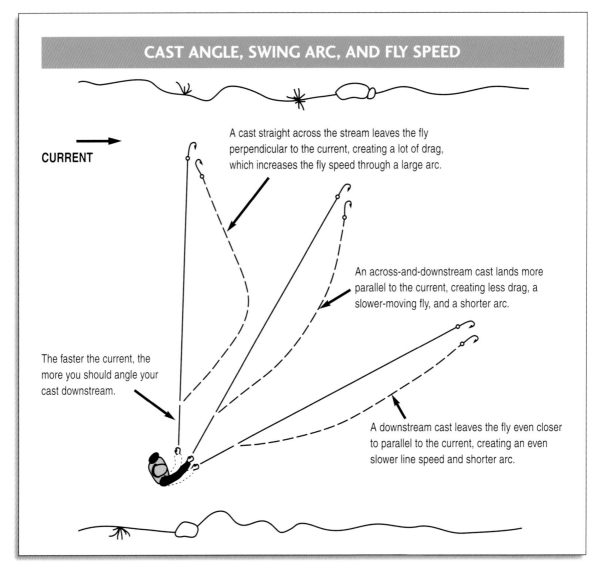

CURRENT

A cast straight across the stream leaves the fly perpendicular to the current, creating a lot of drag, which increases the fly speed through a large arc.

An across-and-downstream cast lands more parallel to the current, creating less drag, a slower-moving fly, and a shorter arc.

The faster the current, the more you should angle your cast downstream.

A downstream cast leaves the fly even closer to parallel to the current, creating an even slower line speed and shorter arc.

an active insect (wet fly) or baitfish (streamer), or the swinging movement of *any* fly simply may trigger a strike response from the trout. On any given day, the truth might be one or the other or anything in between. Fortunately, it's not necessary to know why the trout strikes, but it is important to understand how the current affects the action of the fly

and what you can do to modify or enhance that action.

Most fly fishers are taught that a subsurface tight-line presentation should be made with a quartering across-and-downstream cast. That's a good place to start, but it's more important to keep in mind that wherever you cast it's the *speed* of the swing that's most crucial because it determines the speed of the fly. If the current is fast and you cast more across than downstream, the fly will barely sink at all. You'll see a wake behind it as it motorboats across the water's surface. In most cases, a swing like that won't elicit a strike. It would be better to cast at a greater down-stream angle, causing the fly line to land more closely to parallel with the current. At this casting angle, less fly line is perpendicular to the current, so less drag occurs. Less drag allows the fly to sink a bit before it begins a somewhat slower swing. Although the swing will be shorter, the speed of the fly will be more likely to induce to a strike. Conversely, slower current requires more of an across-stream cast to get the proper fly speed.

The most elusive factor when you are learning tight-line techniques is establishing how fast you want the fly to swim through the water. As a rule, any swing where the fly leaves a wake is probably too fast. Although you might occasionally take a fish on a fast swing, the odds are greater that the fish will strike but miss the fly. A fly that doesn't swing at all or swings so slowly that it's vir-tually inactive in the water probably won't attract too many strikes either. You'll have to experiment with the swing speed in the be-ginning, but it won't take long before you find the sweet spot where the fly sinks a foot or so below the surface and moves at a speed that entices a strike. The trick is to let the trout teach you the correct fly speed. You should always make a point to remember how you presented the fly either when you catch a fish or get a strike and then match that fly speed on subsequent presentations.

An upstream mend reduces drag on the fly line, which will slow the fly down and allow it to sink.
PHOTO BY JANA RUSH

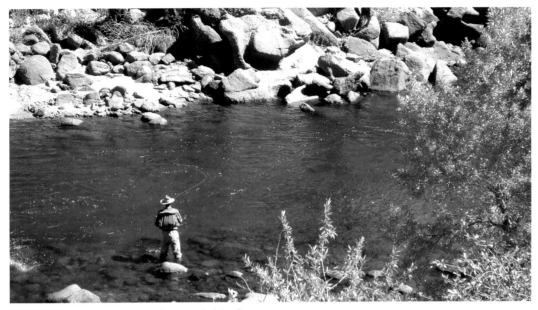

A downstream mend increases the speed of the fly. PHOTO BY JANA RUSH

Change where the swing begins by making an across-and-downstream presentation and then immediately shaking out S curves of slack line. This will cause the fly to dead-drift downstream until the S curves straighten out, at which time the swing will begin. PHOTO BY JANA RUSH

It's also important to note that the sweet spot can change from day to day or in different current conditions.

Once you get the hang of how the angle of your cast to the current affects fly speed, try experimenting with line mends to alter and enhance the fly speed. An upstream line mend reduces drag on the fly line, which will slow fly speed and allow the fly to sink a bit more. Several upstream mends in succession may slow the fly's speed to the point that it's almost at a dead drift. A downstream mend increases the speed of the fly, which is useful in slow-moving water or pools.

You can have additional effect on the fly's depth during the swing by raising or lowering the rod tip. Raising the tip will tend to pull the fly toward the surface. Lowering the tip will help it stay deeper. Don't be afraid to actually hold the rod tip under the water's surface when trying to keep the fly deep.

Sometimes you may not want the fly to begin the swing as soon as it hits the water. You can change where the swing begins by making an across- or across-and-downstream presentation and then immediately shaking out S curves of slack line. The fly will then dead-drift downstream until the S curves straighten out, at which time the swing will begin.

Some tight-line enthusiasts believe that adding action to the fly during the swing increases their odds of getting a strike while others insist that you should not manipulate the fly as it swings. If you choose to animate the fly, consider making long, slow, one- to two-foot strips as the fly swings crosscurrent. Twitches, short strips, and short releases of fly line that allow the fly to momentarily dead-drift may also induce strikes. Some fly fishers

feel a streamer should be stripped faster in clear water and slower in dirty water. A similar practice is advocated for colder water where it sometimes pays to slow the retrieve. Almost all tight liners agree that when the swing ends you should allow the fly to swim in the current for a few moments before beginning the upstream retrieve. That pause will allow a trout that has been chasing the fly to catch it.

The bottom line is that the retrieve is fertile ground for experimentation. If one retrieve doesn't work, mix things up, try something new. And then make a point to remember how you were retrieving the fly when you do get a strike so you can repeat it.

Don't be surprised if you miss more strikes than usual when fishing a tight line. Sometimes the trout simply misses the fly or

Lowering the rod tip and using a strip strike may help if you're consistently missing strikes.
PHOTO BY ANGUS DRUMMOND

TIGHT-LINE RETRIEVE STYLES

Holding the fly line against the cork when retrieving the fly may make it more difficult to detect subtler strikes to slow-swinging flies. PHOTO BY KYLE HENDRICKS

Retrieving the fly line between the thumb and forefinger of the rod hand may make detecting subtler strikes easier. PHOTO BY KYLE HENDRICKS

presentation pulls the fly up and away from the fish. A strip strike doesn't pull the fly up as much, so if the fish does miss it, the fly will still be in the water where it's possible for the trout to strike it again.

A final consideration is the mechanics of how you make your retrieve. Most fly fishers hold the fly line against the cork with their index or middle finger and then strip the line from behind it. It's a retrieve that's stood the test of time, but it may not be the best one for the subtle takes that sometimes occur when tight lining. When I first fished for king salmon, I couldn't believe how subtle the strikes were on slow swings. If you think you need more sensitivity to strikes when you're retrieving the fly, try holding the fly line between your thumb and forefinger on your rod hand rather than against the cork grip. It takes a bit of practice, but once I got used to it I never looked back. I use it all the time now.

WEIGHTED OR UNWEIGHTED FLIES AND SINK-TIP LINES

Traditionally, wet flies and streamers were unweighted, but as fly fishers explored more challenging water types, the need to get fly imitations down quickly led to the increased use of weighted flies. Tight liners now commonly use coneheads, beadheads, and lead wire under the dubbing to get flies down in deep or heavy water conditions. Anglers who feel that an unweighted pattern has better action in the water may choose to add weight to the leader. In most cases, you won't need to modify basic tight-line techniques when you use weighted flies or attach weight to the leader. The weighted flies may require fewer mends to get them

the hook is misaligned and doesn't gain purchase when you strike. When you do miss a strike, it pays to cast back to the exact same swing line—sometimes the trout will hit the fly again. If you find that you are consistently missing strikes, consider lowering the rod tip during the swing and using a strip strike. Striking with the rod on a tight-line

down deep, but the fly speed principles remain the same.

Some streamer fishermen lengthen the leader to as much as 10 feet when they fish a weighted pattern on a floating line. They then cast the fly across and slightly upstream where the longer leader and an upstream mend or two allows it to quickly sink. It's an especially useful technique for slow to moderate current speeds where the water depth is four feet or less, although it does take a bit of practice to get used to casting a weighted fly on a long leader.

Streamer fishing often requires sink-tip or full sinking fly lines, particularly for big water. Unlike a weighted fly that might well up in heavier current when fished on a floating line, a sink-tip or full sinking line keeps the fly close to the bottom for much of the swing and during the retrieve. It's important to stick to a short 3- to 4-foot leader when you fish a sink-tip or full sinking line. The shorter leader will help keep the fly from welling up into the water column. You might also notice that the swing is a bit more sluggish when you fish a sink-tip or full sinking line, but that's a good thing because it means a slower fly speed. You can alter the fly speed of a sinking-line presentation by changing the angle of your cast or raising or lowering

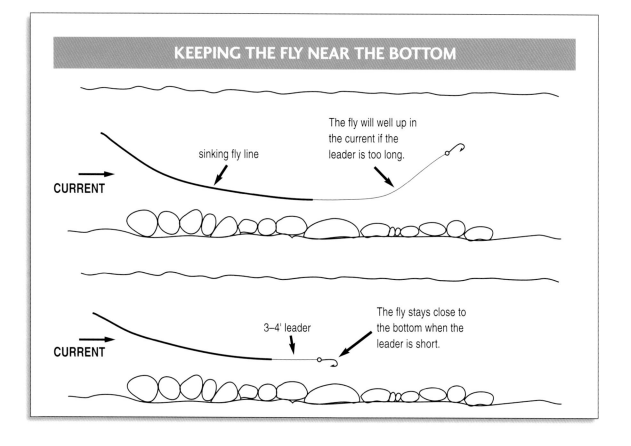

KEEPING THE FLY NEAR THE BOTTOM

sinking fly line

The fly will well up in the current if the leader is too long.

CURRENT

3–4' leader

The fly stays close to the bottom when the leader is short.

CURRENT

the rod tip. Although a mend will alter the fly speed, it can be more difficult to execute, especially with a full sinking line.

Aside from a sometimes surprisingly delicate take in slower water, streamer fishing is a pretty violent business—trout hit a moving fly hard. For that reason, tippets need not be lighter than 2X or 3X, and if you're fishing weighted flies, you probably could get by without a tapered leader in most applications. You may want to lighten up the tippet a bit more when fishing smaller wet flies, although tippet size doesn't seem to be as critical when fishing a tight line as it is when fishing a dry fly.

TACKLE FOR TIGHT LINERS

Before 1960, slower-action bamboo fly rods were often marketed as having a wet-fly action. At the time, wet-fly fishermen thought a slow, full-flex action made the rod easier to roll cast. The assumption was that a roll cast would keep the unweighted wet flies wetter, and thus more likely to sink, than if they were air dried with a false cast. Today, tight-line fly fishers typically prefer 9-foot or longer graphite rods because the longer, stiffer rods make mending the fly line easier. Any problem they might have keeping the subsurface flies wet is solved by simply adding weight to the fly or leader or mending line to allow the fly more time to sink.

Tight-line fly patterns fall into two basic groups—attractor style and match-the-baitfish or in some cases match-the-emerging-hatch styles. Today's attractor-style streamer patterns typically don't match any particular trout food but most probably incorporate some trigger that is associated with a trout food. Those triggers include

The Muddler Minnow (left) imitates a sculpin. The Woolly Bugger is an attractor-style streamer that doesn't imitate anything in particular.

It's important to carry streamer imitations in a variety of colors and color combinations. The color of the fly is often more important than a specific fly pattern.

large eyes, flashy materials, lifelike rabbit-strips, and contrasting shades of color. In the 1960s there was a movement toward tying streamer patterns that matched actual bait-fish. The Thunder Creek series, Muddler Minnow, and sculpin imitations come to mind as classic examples. There are good reasons to match baitfish, and you still find some tight liners who only fish patterns that match their local trout foods.

Probably the best approach, at least to streamer fishing, is to incorporate a little of both worlds in your fly selection. You can never go wrong with a few Muddler Min-nows or sculpin imitations. For attractor-style streamers, make sure you have some small sizes and a variety of color combina-tions. You should have both weighted and unweighted copies of your patterns. When

fishing new water, always inquire about local streamer patterns. You'll often find that, rather than a particular pattern, a color com-bination is popular. The best attractor-style streamer patterns often incorporate color contrast, which makes sense if you look at most baitfish. They tend to be dark on top and lighter on the bottom or have stripes of contrasting color.

Although it's fun to agonize over streamer patterns, the trout often care less than the fisherman. The odds are if you pick a pattern and fish it well, you'll get strikes. If you don't get strikes, then it's time to try some-thing different. It may be useful to develop a system where you try dark patterns and then light patterns or some other variations just because it breaks up the routine and keeps things interesting. You may find in the end

The Homer Rhode loop knot or a similar loop knot may allow a streamer to be more active and lifelike.

A match-the-hatch imitation of an ascending pupa or nymph, such as this LaFontaine Emergent Sparkle Caddisfly Pupa, can be deadly when fished with tight-line methods.

that discovering the water type where the trout are holding is ultimately more important than the fly pattern, but fooling around with different patterns, swing speeds, and retrievals never hurts until you make that discovery.

Tight liners can spend hours talking about how to tie the fly to the tippet. I usually use a Homer Rhode loop knot, which some anglers believe allows the fly to be more active, but in a pinch I'm not opposed to the tried-and-true improved clinch knot.

Wet-fly selection has a surprising number of similarities to streamer selection. Once again, many wets work the trigger side more than the match-the-hatch side of the coin. Soft hackles are a good bet because they incorporate an active hackle and bright general-purpose attractor colors or they can be tied with a match-the-hatch colored body. Most recently, beadhead-style nymphs with or without a soft hackle have been used effectively with tight-line techniques. Match-the-hatch beadheads often prove deadly as do old attractor-style favorites such as the Prince Nymph. Finally, don't forget there will be times when you *do* have to match an ascending pupa or nymph to be effective with a wet fly. The best example of effective match-the-hatch subsurface flies is Gary LaFontaine's sparkle caddis series. These patterns are killer when dead-drifted or fished with tight-line methods.

ADVANCED SUBSURFACE TIGHT-LINE TECHNIQUES

An amazing body of fly-fishing literature is devoted to fishing the tight line. In the past, most of the attention was given to wet-fly techniques, but more recently streamer tactics have dominated. I think that for the most part the real work on how to fish and manage a tight line was completed in the 1970s, but you'll still see an occasional magazine article that presents a "new" technique that on closer examination turns out to be a new variation of a standard tight-line method. The truth is that for most fishing situations you just can't go wrong sticking with basic tight-line techniques, but occa-sionally there is a need for something a little different.

Most advanced tight-line techniques apply standard tight-line tactics to atypical water types or add a specific action to the fly during retrieval. Here are several interesting examples.

Downstream Mend

When a trout is holding tight against the opposite bank, sometimes a standard across-and-downstream tight-line presentation isn't practical. In this situation, make an across-stream cast against the opposite bank that lands upstream from where you've spotted the fish or believe a fish might be holding.

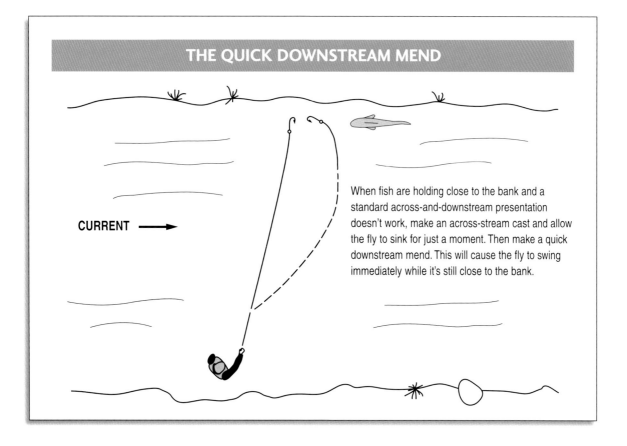

THE QUICK DOWNSTREAM MEND

CURRENT ⟶

When fish are holding close to the bank and a standard across-and-downstream presentation doesn't work, make an across-stream cast and allow the fly to sink for just a moment. Then make a quick downstream mend. This will cause the fly to swing immediately while it's still close to the bank.

When the fly lands on the water, allow it to sink for just a moment and then make a quick *downstream* mend. This will cause the fly to begin swinging immediately while it's still close against the bank.

Strip, Strip, Wiggle, Wiggle

Numerous tight-line techniques use rod movements to stutter or stop the fly during the swing so that it's easier for the trout to take it. One uncomplicated technique for moderate current speed uses an across- or across-and-slightly-downstream presentation. As soon as the swing begins, give the fly two or three short, fast strips and then wiggle the rod tip parallel to the water's surface. The wiggles create just enough slack to slow down or stutter the fly's movement and pre-cipitate a crashing strike.

Two Streamers

Some fly fishers use two streamers. It can be a deadly combination, and I don't mean that in terms of casting the two-fly rig, which does require a degree of caution. It's best to use one bright fly and one darker fly. The flies can be the same size, but I prefer a larger fly trailed by a smaller second fly. Use a clinch knot tied to the bend of hook with 12 to 18 inches of 2X to 4X leader material to attach the second fly. Another option is to use a soft hackle or beadhead nymph as the second fly. It seems like the larger, first fly often gets the trout's attention and induces it to strike the second, smaller fly.

Greased-Line Method

You will sometimes hear a tight liner refer to the greased-line method. This technique was

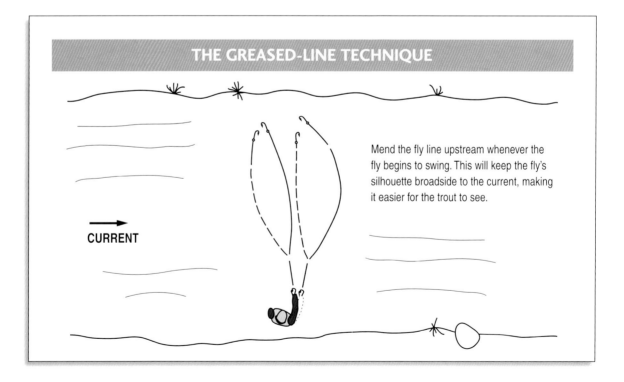

THE GREASED-LINE TECHNIQUE

CURRENT

Mend the fly line upstream whenever the fly begins to swing. This will keep the fly's silhouette broadside to the current, making it easier for the trout to see.

Make a stack mend by shaking extra fly line out with an up-and-down vertical motion of the rod. Use the stack mend to make the fly sink deeper or assist a dead drift. PHOTO BY ANGUS DRUMMOND

originally developed by salmon fishermen to present a fly's silhouette broadside to the salmon with a natural drift. Trout fishermen modified the classic greased-line technique as applied to salmon for fishing streamers to trout. It's basically an exaggeration of the same technique you would use to slow down the speed that a streamer swings or to get it down deeper. Start by casting across and upstream and then begin making upstream mends whenever necessary to prevent the floating fly line from swinging the fly. If you keep these mends coming in a timely fashion and follow the fly's progress downstream with the rod, the fly will drift sideways to the current, which means it will present its silhouette to the trout.

If you find that you're having trouble keeping the fly from swinging at the very beginning of the presentation, you may have to throw a few stack mends to get the fly down. The term "stack mend" is used to describe a variety of ways to shake out additional fly line to either assist a dead drift or, as in this case, allow a fly to sink more quickly. The most efficient way to make a stack mend is to strip some additional line off the reel before you make the cast, and then when you make the cast, shake that extra line out by moving the rod tip back and forth vertically, similar to the way many of us were taught to shake out S curves of slack line except that you move the rod vertically rather than horizontally. Once you get the hang of the stack mend, you'll find that the slack line will move out in loops that resemble little roll casts. The stack mends will be most effective if you hold the rod high and try to get the loops of slack line closer to the fly rather than closer to the rod tip.

A number of years ago, the greased-line technique was thought to be *the* answer for fishing a streamer to trout. All you heard about was getting the fly broadside so the trout could see it. You don't hear as much about it nowadays, but it's still a good technique to have in your bag of tricks. I think it works better with an unweighted or lightly weighed fly in moderate current that is not broken up by lots of in-stream barriers or variations in depth.

Lifts

I sometimes overhear a middle-age nymph fisherman talking about the Leisenring Lift in close to reverential tones, although you seldom see any of them actually practicing it on the stream. These are most often the nymph fishermen who were weaned on short- or long-line nymphing tactics where a dead drift was crucial. The idea of the Leisenring Lift was both seductive and heretical because the most important part of the lift requires a tight line.

In practice, the Leisenring Lift, at least the way Jim Leisenring did it, required a pretty specific set of conditions. He needed a stretch of water about fifteen feet or longer that was about two or three feet deep, *and* he needed to be able to spot a trout in that water. Once those conditions were met, Leisenring positioned himself so that he could cast an unweighted nymph upstream and across from the trout. The fly had to be cast far enough upstream to allow it to sink to the bottom before it traveled downstream to the trout. The key to the technique was to allow little or no slack in the fly line or leader, but not enough tension to alter the natural drift of the fly. As the fly drifted downstream Leisenring followed it with the rod tip to maintain the delicate no slack/no tension ratio until it was about four feet or so upstream of the trout, at which point he stopped the rod. Since there was little or no slack in the line and leader when the rod was checked, the current would slowly lift the fly toward the surface, creating the illusion of an actively swimming or emerging nymph. It was a deadly technique, especially at the beginning of a hatch.

Frank Sawyer, the renowned British spring creek river keeper and nympher, developed a similar method that he called the induced take. Sawyer's technique differed from Leisenring's because he would actually lift his rod to manipulate the fly. Of course, the downside of either of these lift methods was that you needed to spot a feeding trout or at least fish a lie that you had a pretty good idea would hold a fish. The upside was that fishing these lifts was as close to the excitement of dry-fly fishing as you can get below the surface.

There is one final benefit of the mythical lifts. It has allowed modern day nymphers to think outside of the dead-drift box. They let their flies swing up at the end of a drift and make modifications of that swing with line mends. Even more important is that it made nymphers aware of a subtle sweet spot between tight lining and the dead drift where it's easier to detect strikes and still achieve a natural drift even if you're using a weighted fly.

A tactic with similarities to a lift is described by Dave Hughes in his book *Wet Flies* as the Hidy Subsurface Swing. Dave actually coined the method as the Hidy Subsurface Swing because he learned it from

Jim Leisenring's disciple Pete Hidy. The sub-surface swing has its roots in several wet-fly and dry-fly techniques, but Hidy refined it for use with flymphs, which are essentially nymph imitations that are tied with spikey fur and guard hair bodies designed to trap air when pulled under the water's surface. The trapped air bubbles give the fly a sparkly appearance that resembles that of an emerging caddisfly pupa and, to a lesser degree, other emerging aquatic insects. Hidy fished the flymph like a wet fly on a tight line rather than dead-drifting it as nymphs are now commonly fished.

To execute Hidy's subsurface swing, position yourself thirty to fifty feet upstream or upstream and across from a rising trout. Once in position, present the fly two to three feet to the side of the trout's feeding lane and two to three feet upstream from it.

The idea is to place the fly where the current will swing it into the feeding lane of the trout. It is crucial to pull the fly under-water when it lands by lifting the rod tip. Once the fly is below the surface, lower the rod tip to allow it to swing in a slow-moving arc over the trout. If you don't pull the fly under, it will stay on the surface and spook the trout when it motorboats over its nose.

Typically the strike is not aggressive. You'll just feel the line tighten. When this happens, remember that you've made a downstream presentation and you need to slightly delay the strike to overcome the adverse hooking characteristics that go along with an upstream casting position. Waiting that extra moment to strike can be especially difficult when you see a bulge of water as the trout turns on the fly.

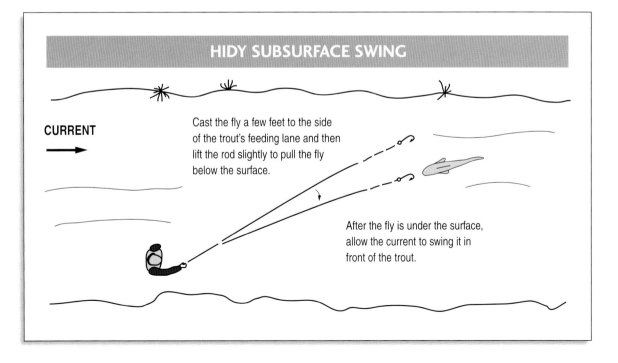

HIDY SUBSURFACE SWING

CURRENT

Cast the fly a few feet to the side of the trout's feeding lane and then lift the rod slightly to pull the fly below the surface.

After the fly is under the surface, allow the current to swing it in front of the trout.

Hidy's subsurface swing works best on flats where the flow is uniform and not too swift. It's like Leisenring's lift in the sense that you need to find a specific water type to apply the method to if you want good results. It also takes some practice to find the best spot to place the fly for an optimal swing. Until you dial it in, it's better to err on the conservative side and place the fly a little higher upstream on your first cast rather than cast too far and put the trout down. Remember that if the fly isn't taken, allow it to swing well away from the fish before you pick up to avoid spooking it.

Hidy's technique was designed for wet flies and specifically for flymphs, but the subsurface swing does lend itself to tweaking. I've actually used it to fish smaller unweighted streamers in front of rocks where I thought a trout might lie.

You may be wondering how the subsurface swing connects to lifts, but if you look at the elements of both techniques, you'll see they have several components in common. Both are best used when you spot a trout, and both use the current to subtly lift or swing the fly. The subsurface swing uses the current to slide the fly in an arc across the surface while the Leisenring Lift uses the current to lift the fly in an arc vertically from the stream bottom toward the surface.

TIGHT-LINING DRY FLIES

Fishing a dry fly on a tight line isn't as off-the-wall as you might think. Most fly fishermen have tried skittering or somehow activating an Elk Hair Caddis on the water's surface. But for many dry-fly fishermen, tight lining happens almost by accident because most of them think they're doing

something wrong if they don't get a drag-free drift. And that's often the case, but there is a time and a place for the tight line when fishing a dry fly. It may even be time to consider tight-line dry-fly fishing as a legitimate system of techniques that has a place in everyone's bag of tricks. Here are a few ideas to get you started.

Drag-Free, Skitter-Swing, and Drown

This is just a fancy name for what many of us already do when we fish an Elk Hair Caddis. You start by making an across-and-upstream cast and allowing the fly to dead-drift. When the fly gets to the point where it begins to drag, you lift the rod tip and skitter it for a bit. Once the swing really begins to kick in, you give the line a little tug to pull the fly under the surface. When the fly, which is now essentially a subsurface emerger/attractor pattern, swings to a position directly downstream from you, let it hang in the current for a moment and then either strip it back upstream like you would a streamer or pick it up and recast.

This technique works best with stout, buoyant flies such as Elk Hair Caddis or Stimulators, but in slower-moving water I have pulled delicate little parachutes and CDC patterns under the surface and caught trout. Most fly fishers I've talked to can tell stories about how they left a dry fly dragging downstream below them while trying to figure out what to do next, only to have a trout take it. The lesson here, of course, is if your accidents, mistakes, or inattention results in strikes, incorporate that into your strategy.

And once again, remember that for any fly fished on a tight line that is swinging downstream from you, it's important to delay the strike just a hair. If you react to the strike too quickly, you will botch the hookup.

HIGH-STICKING DRY FLIES

Fly fishers most often associate high-sticking with the short-line, dead-drift tactics employed by nymph fishermen. What they may not realize is that dry-fly fishermen were using high-stick techniques to improve their chances for drag-free drifts long before high-sticking nymphs was popularized in the 1970s.

Dapping

Dapping is one of the oldest forms of high-sticking a dry fly. Historically, dappers used 12- to 18-foot-long rods with the line attached to the end. A stiff-hackled dry fly was tied to the end of the line and allowed to skitter and bounce on the water's surface as it blew in the wind. Although dapping isn't practiced with the same tackle or even the same techniques as it was in earlier centuries, it's still a useful dry-fly tactic nowadays.

Once in position, carefully move the fly rod out over the stream. Drop the fly on to the water well downstream of the trout, and let it drift with the current until the leader tightens. Use a roll cast motion to cast it upstream.

When the fly begins its downstream drift, hold as much fly line off the water as possible.

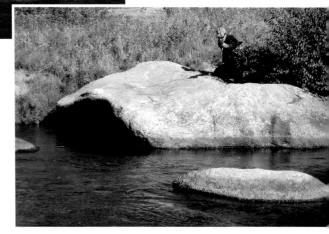

Continue the drift downstream, and if you don't get a strike, recast when the fly begins to drag in the current.

The simplest form of modern dapping requires stealth and patience. You should target water within a rod's length of the stream bank where you have seen a trout rise or where you expect trout to be holding. You must then make an approach to a position on the stream bank where you will be able to hold the fly rod out over the water and dangle the dry fly down to the surface. The imitation can be dead-drifted or allowed to dance and skitter on the surface as it blows in the breeze. On calm days, activate the fly with the rod by dapping it on the surface in a way that imitates aquatic insect behavior.

There are several things you need to do if you want to become a successful dapper. First, you should slowly and carefully approach the trout from downstream. Pay special attention to keeping a low profile by crouching down or even crawling if necessary. In addition, you should try to use streamside vegetation to break up your silhouette and hide your approach whenever possible.

Once you are in position on the stream bank, the most delicate part of successful dapping is moving the fly rod into position without spooking the trout. There are a couple of ways you can accomplish this. For spooky fish in slow-moving, clear water, hold the fly in your hand while you move the fly rod very slowly out over the water with the tip pointing downstream from the trout's position. The rod should be low and parallel to the water's surface. In most cases, you won't need much more than a rod length of leader/fly line extending past the tip-top guide. Remember that the less line you have out, the less chance it has to tangle in the streamside vegetation.

Once you have the rod out over the water with the tip pointing downstream, slowly raise it to a vertical position. If the breeze is favorable, you can simply release the fly over the water and use the breeze to carry it upstream to the fish and then bounce and dance it on the surface. If conditions are calm, gently toss the fly on to the water's surface downstream from the fish. Then let the fly drift until the leader tightens in the current and flip it upstream of the fish with a roll-cast motion (this is very similar to the water-tension cast nymphers use to flip a weighted fly upstream). Once the fly begins drifting down to the fish, hold the rod high with as little slack in the line as possible. At this point you can either dead-drift the fly or activate it.

If the trout are holding in a more forgiving lie such as a riffle that hides your movements, you may be able to just hold the rod out over the water's surface, drop the fly upstream from the fish, and let it drift downstream. Some fly fishers prefer to use all leader when they dap while others believe that having a few feet of fly line extending out past the tip-top guide helps them better control the fly.

Although today's shorter fly rods limit the range of dapping tactics, it's still a very productive technique for smaller streams where backcasts are hindered by brush or trees and is surprisingly effective on skittish trout close to the banks on hard-fished tailwaters or spring creeks. It's sometimes even possible to apply your dapping skills to trout that are rising nearby when you're in a midriver casting position.

High-Sticking a Dry Fly

Dry-fly fishermen often practice other types of high-sticking without even realizing it. The most common example is when there is fast-moving water between you and a

High-sticking a dry fly when there is fast water between you and the rising trout helps prevent drag.

trout that's rising in a slower moving current. If you make a standard across-and-upstream presentation, the fly will begin to drag the moment the fly line lands on the faster-moving water. But if you make your across-and-upstream cast and then hold the rod high, you'll be able to lift the fly line off the faster-moving water and allow the fly to continue its downstream drift without drag.

In another variation, you can add precious moments of drag-free drift to a dry-fly presentation by simply raising the rod toward end of the drift when the fly line begins to drag. Raising the rod lifts fly line off the water's surface, which is the most common cause of drag at the end of the drift. In addition, you can use the high rod to activate the fly pattern near the end of the drift when the line tightens. Raising the rod allows the fly to skitter and jump on the surface rather than getting pulled under the

water on the swing. This type of high-sticking is especially effective when using high-riding fly patterns such as the Elk Hair Caddis, Stimulator, or Bivisible that can be made to skitter and jump over the surface in a manner similar to a dapped fly. This action closely imitates the erratic flight of an egg-laying female caddisfly or other insect that is active on the water's surface. You can also high-stick a high-riding dry-fly pattern on a tight line at the end of the drift, causing it to sweep across the current in an erratic, strike-producing arc.

If, conversely, you'd rather get a few more feet of drag-free drift at the end of the drift, simply lower the rod from the high-stick position. This will add a bit of slack line to the drift, which should allow the fly to float drag-free a little longer.

Once you understand the advantages of using the fly rod to lift the fly line off the

HIGH-STICKING A DRY FLY IN A FAST-WATER SEAM

Cast across and upstream. Hold the rod high as soon as the fly lands to keep as much fly line off the water as possible.

Follow the dry fly with the rod tip as it drifts downstream. If necessary, raise the rod tip a bit more to control slack line.

As the fly drifts farther downstream, lower the rod tip to feed slack into the drift.

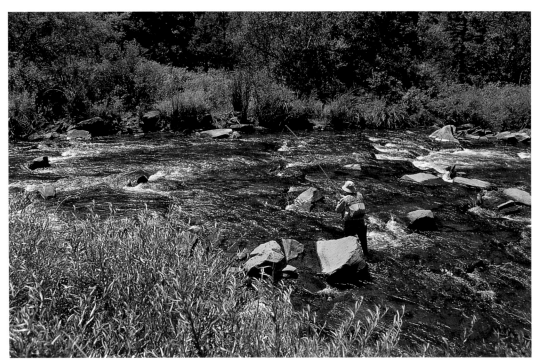

High-sticking a dry fly is an ideal technique for pocketwater.

water to avoid drag or extend a drag-free drift, you'll realize there are countless variations that can help you achieve better dry-fly drifts. If you've ever tried to employ a standard across-and-upstream dry-fly presentation in pocketwater, you know that it's virtually impossible to get a drag-free drift. High-sticking the dry fly through the pockets is the perfect solution.

The key to pocketwater success is to position yourself close enough to where the trout are holding to enable you to hold all or most of your fly line off the water. You should carefully approach pocketwater from downstream or across stream to avoid accidentally spooking fish, but don't be scared to get up close and personal. The characteristic turbulence of pocketwater provides ideal cover for a close approach. Although the nature of pocketwater doesn't allow very long drifts, high-sticking techniques can buy you the foot or so of drag-free drift that is all you need to pound up a strike. Once you get the hang of high-sticking the pockets, you'll find trout in places as small as saucer-sized slicks—where all you need are a few inches of drag-free drift and it's fish on!

Fishing the Waking Fly

Waking flies are most often associated with steelhead or salmon fishing, but the same techniques can also be applied to trout fishing. Once again, trout fishermen often learn by mistake about the power of a waking fly to attract strikes. The most common example occurs when a deer-hair style grasshopper

Alaskan anglers fish deer-hair mouse patterns downstream and wake the fly by lifting the rod tip a few inches and then dropping it, causing the fly to create a gentle wake in the current.

Fishing a mouse pattern with waking techniques is highly effective on arctic char in Alaska.

pattern is allowed to drift downstream while a fisherman is briefly preoccupied with other concerns. During that time the hopper drags in the current, creating a wake, and a trout simply comes up and quietly takes the fly.

That sort of experience will lead an attentive fly fisher to incorporate this kind of waking fly action into his strategy for the day. It's as easy as casting the hopper pattern downstream and fishing it like you would a flymph on a subsurface swing, but rather than pulling the fly under the surface you gently pull it upstream a few inches by lifting the rod tip and then lowering the rod a bit and lifting it again as the fly swings in a slow arc across the current. The gentle lifts, of course, cause the fly to create a wake on the water's surface.

The waking-fly strategy you hear the most about uses deer-hair mouse patterns on large brown trout after dark or for big rainbow trout or arctic char in Alaska. The trick to the technique is to have a fly pattern that will wake rather than skitter across the surface when you lift it. You also need to find the kind of uniform slow- to moderate-speed current that allows the waking action to be most effective. As it turns out, any fly pattern that creates a wake rather than diving under the surface or skittering over it when the line tightens may induce a trout to strike.

Loch-Style High-Sticking for Trout

An interesting high-sticking twist has its origins in an Irish Loch-fishing style where a dry-fly imitation of a local mayfly is fished with a gang of three wet flies trailed behind it. The wet flies, which imitate various emerging stages of the mayfly, are rigged about three feet apart. A 10-foot or longer fly rod is used to fish the setup off the wind-ward side of a boat, which is allowed to drift broadside to the breeze. The angler animates his flies by lifting the dry fly up off the water's surface and bouncing and activating it. The gang of three flies below the dry fly acts as an anchor to keep the dry fly from blowing completely off the water's surface. Activating the dry fly in this way often induces a strike and serves the double duty of adding life to the wet flies, which imitate emerging forms of the adult.

The less involved American version of the technique uses a buoyant dry fly such as a

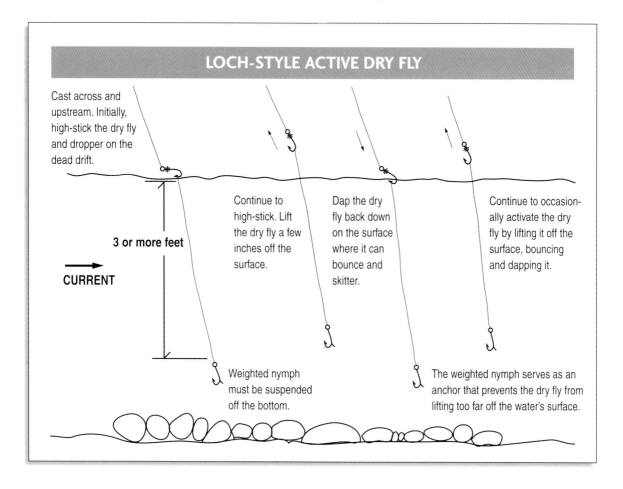

LOCH-STYLE ACTIVE DRY FLY

Cast across and upstream. Initially, high-stick the dry fly and dropper on the dead drift.

3 or more feet

CURRENT

Continue to high-stick. Lift the dry fly a few inches off the surface.

Dap the dry fly back down on the surface where it can bounce and skitter.

Continue to occasionally activate the dry fly by lifting it off the surface, bouncing and dapping it.

Weighted nymph must be suspended off the bottom.

The weighted nymph serves as an anchor that prevents the dry fly from lifting too far off the water's surface.

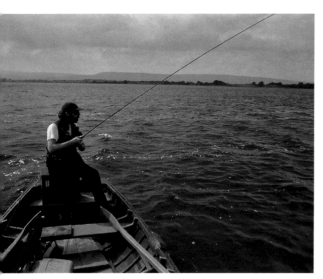

Irish loch–style fly fishing employs a type of high-sticking using a dry fly and wet flies.

Nothing beats the way a trout slams a streamer just before it straightens on the swing.

Stimulator, Elk Hair Caddis, or Wulff with a weighted nymph trailed three feet or more below it. You should rig the trailing nymph so that it is suspended above, rather than bounced along, the streambed. Next, cast the setup across and upstream in the same manner you fish a hopper/dropper rig, but after a short dead drift try high-sticking to tighten the leader and then activate the dry fly by occasionally bouncing and dancing it on the surface. The weighted nymph on the longer-than-normal trailer supplies the anchor to keep the fly from being pulled completely off the surface. The active dry fly tends to induce strikes as does the active, darting nymph. Some fly fishers take the tactic a step further by trailing two weighted nymphs or beadheads when fishing in deeper water.

You may have noticed a common thread running through the techniques presented in this chapter. That thread occurred to me a number of years ago when I realized how much I used tight-line tactics in conjunction with drag-free techniques. The tight-line stuff, though, was almost always an afterthought added at the end of a drift or a simple mistake. When I began to understand that there were times when tight-line strategies could catch fish when a dead drift couldn't, I started to take them more seriously and incorporate them into my fishing routine.

I think at heart I'll always prefer the elegance of a fly fished with a drag-free drift if for no other reason than the way a trout takes it, but I also know there is this whole other tight-line world to back me up. And besides, it's kind of fun when a trout slams that streamer just before it straightens on the swing. . . .

CHAPTER 4

Meadow Streams

Dry fly and streamer tactics for meadow water, whatever the season

"Meadow stream" can mean a lot of things. Most fly fishers will agree with a definition that features a luxurious vision of mostly flat water slowly meandering through a grassy valley bottom. Where riffle water does occur, it's typically rolling, although you will occasionally see whitewater in breaks. Meadow streams often lack the in-stream rocks that create pocketwater in a faster-flowing freestone stream. The main current line is sometimes subtle, perhaps indicated only by the downstream movement of bubbles or flecks of foam. Meandering meadow streams often form numerous bends, twists, and turns. A section of water measured one mile long as the crow flies may actually be five miles of meanders on the ground.

I look for spring runoff to deeply undercut meandering meadow stream banks and in the process create superlative habitat for large trout. Low-growing grasses or sagebrush often surrounds classic meadow streams, but don't rule out occasional thickets of willow or other brush along the banks.

You might also consider the term "meadow stream" itself as a bit of a misnomer. Most meadow streams are actually sections of meadow water where a faster-flowing freestone stream encounters the flatter gradient of a valley floor. An increase in gradient upstream or downstream of the valley will cause the stream to revert to its freestone nature. Comparatively few rivers or streams feature meadow water for their entire length. Beyond this basic description, there are several notable distinctions you can make between various types of meadow water.

MEADOW WATER TYPES

A tailwater meadow stream occurs below a reservoir. Most likely it started off as an

Most tailwater meadow streams were probably unregulated meadow streams before the dam was built, but afterwards, they took on some tailwater characteristics, too.

unregulated meadow stream before the dam was built on it, but afterward chances are that it has taken on some tailwater characteristics too. The aquatic insect life is probably less diverse than it would be in an unregulated meadow stream, but the insects that do live there thrive. There are likely to be large populations of the smaller mayfly species such as Tricos, Blue-Winged Olives, Pale Morning Duns, or Sulphurs. You may even see some *Callibaetis* that have migrated down from the reservoir. The number of midges is astronomical. Non-insect trout foods such as scuds, sow bugs, or aquatic annelids may also be present because the unique tailwater environment allows them to be. For fly fishers, this abundance of trout foods means that there will probably be more trout and larger trout. And those trout will most likely be more selective about what they eat.

Spring creek meadow water has a number of characteristics in common with tailwater meadow streams. In addition, the constancy of spring creek water temperatures is ideal for growing trout and the food that trout eat. Classic spring creek meadow water is gin clear (or for that matter, vodka clear) most of the time and will probably have more aquatic vegetation than most tailwater meadow streams. On average, it may have fewer riffles than any of the other types of meadow streams. Spring creek meadow water trout are legendary for their feeding selectivity and the technical difficulties inherent in making a presentation to water that is flat, clear, and unblemished by any surface features that might hide the fly line or leader from the trout.

The final type of meadow stream is just plain old, unregulated, wild meadow water.

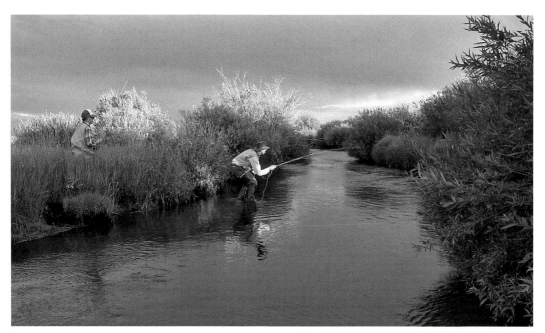

Classic meadow streams are often surrounded by low-growing grasses, but don't rule out occasional thickets of willow or other brush along the banks.

Spring creek meadow streams have very clear water and fewer riffles than other meadow water types.

It's the meadow stream that was there before any dams were constructed. It's a stream that probably depends more on spring runoff as a water source than an underground spring, although if you get far enough downstream from the source on a spring creek meadow stream, it will begin to fish a lot like wild meadow water. Wild meadow water often has a preponderance of undercut banks that are carved out annually by the unregulated spring runoff. Although it is capable of supporting a good population of trout and has the habitat that larger trout require, wild meadow water is often less productive than tailwater or spring creek meadow streams.

Surprisingly, the fact that wild meadow water is less productive is what charms me the most. It means that you won't find a trout every place you think one should be and you may find a few where you definitely think they shouldn't be. I also like the idea that you may have to get off the beaten path just a bit to even find wild meadow water. That means hiking into the backcountry where there is the promise of a meandering stretch of water that may be no more than five or ten feet wide. Or maybe you'll need to drive a trace road through a seemingly endless number of gates before you get a glimpse of a gorgeous stretch of meadow water snaking its way across a broad valley.

Finally, and this may be scary to some of you tailwater and spring creek freaks, I like wild meadow water because it's typically *not* technical fishing. The aquatic insect species available to trout in wild meadow waters can be diverse, but with a few exceptions the actual populations of each species will not be especially large. Factors affecting this diversity include geographical region, local water chemistry, and the origin of the meadow stream. But the bottom line is that on a typical day wild meadow water is custom-made for attractor-style fly patterns.

I'll admit that when I first started fishing wild meadow water I was pretty much a match-the-hatch techie. It was an understandable approach if you consider I'd spent years fishing the tailwater meadow streams below reservoirs before I decided maybe I should check out what's *above* the reservoir. And I can say that for the most part matching the hatch there worked alright, but I can also say that my style quickly evolved into a more freewheeling, fast-moving approach that required lightening my load. The first thing to go was my overloaded tailwater/spring creek fly-fishing vest.

FISHING WILD MEADOW WATER

Nowadays, my standard strategy for fishing wild meadow water entails carrying a single fly box stocked with various sizes of Elk Hair Caddis, Stimulators, parachute-style dry flies, traditionally hackled dry-fly attractor flies, grasshoppers, beetles, ants, beadhead and weighted nymphs, and a few weighted Woolly Buggers. I said standard strategy because I do make some changes for seasonal eccentricities that we'll talk about later. But no matter what the variations are, it always comes down to a single fly box that I stow in a butt pack with a few spools of 3X to 5X tippet material, an extra $7\frac{1}{2}$-foot long knotless leader, and nippers. Sometimes I wear breathable waders or hippers, but I'll wade wet if the conditions allow it.

This stripped-down meadow water blitzkrieg style revolves around the idea of covering lots of water, seeing what happens,

If possible, it's best to not wade when fishing meadow water.

and then moving on if nothing does. It's a lot like the way you might fish your favorite upland small stream. If there is any kind of a standard vision about what a typical wild meadow stream day should be, it almost always includes a deliciously lazy summer day where you start off fishing a hopper imitation.

Due to some personal idiosyncrasies, I prefer smaller hopper patterns in the size 12 range. Other alternatives include a yellow Stimulator, which pretty much passes for a hopper, or a size 12 or 14 Parachute Hare's Ear tied on a long-shank hook.

A Parachute Hare's Ear tied on a long-shank hook is a good general-purpose meadow stream dry-fly imitation that passes for a hopper, mayfly dun, and assorted other insects.

The fundamental tactic is to cast the hopper up close to the opposite bank and see what happens. As a rule, you should be in a casting position that allows you to get a drag-free drift, although once in a while a little drag or a twitch will actually induce a strike. I don't wade at all on smaller meadow streams, and when I do wade I'm careful to stick to hard-bottom areas. The sand and muck in deposition zones can literally suck you in and at best you'll muddy up the water and yourself.

If possible, I make across-and-upstream or across-and-downstream presentations. Sometimes the nature of a meadow stream will not allow this. Your very best slack-line presentation may not be enough to prevent drag on a fly cast into the ribbon of slower moving water or the current eddies that are often located close to the bank. In those cases, I wade across the stream and cast straight up along the bank or make a downstream presentation. When making same-side presentations, I remind myself that if I do get a strike, it's important to play the fish out from the bank and into open water. If you allow a trout to dart back under a cut bank, you stand a good chance of losing it.

An especially spooky trout may require a grass cast where the fly line lands on the grass or gravel and just the fly and leader land on the water. When the trout strikes, lift the rod up high to get the line off the grass where it might tangle when the fish is played. I often find myself employing this sneaky tactic on smaller meadow streams when I actually cast across the thin strip of land where a meander turns back 180 degrees on itself.

Casting straight upstream along the bank is the best option for getting a drag-free drift in the tricky currents that are sometimes encountered along a meadow stream bank. PHOTO BY KYLE HENDRICKS

Use an across-and-upstream cast to get a grasshopper imitation as close as possible to the opposite bank. Fine-tune the presentation by softly casting the hopper up on the bank and then pulling it back into the water. PHOTO BY KYLE HENDRICKS

An across-and-downstream presentation may be the best option for situations where standard upstream casts cause the fly to drag or when spooky meadow stream trout are encountered. PHOTO BY KYLE HENDRICKS

Spooky trout feeding in shallow riffles near the bank may require a grass cast where the fly line lands on gravel or grass and just the leader and fly land on water. PHOTO BY KYLE HENDRICKS

You can fine-tune the close-to-the-bank hopper cast to include softly casting the fly right up on the grass and then gently pulling it into the water. This gets the fly even closer to the bank, and just the act of pulling it into the water sometimes triggers a strike. A beetle, ant, or even an Elk Hair Caddis works equally well when pulled softly from the bank into the water.

Casting to the slow-moving water against the bank is about as seductive as it gets, especially when it looks like an undercut may be hiding a larger-than-average trout, but don't forget the rest of the stream. Some pretty good fish may be finning over the gravel that's often present just upstream from a bend. Actually, any riffle or current over gravel no matter how deep it is may hold trout. Don't forget the drops into the deeper holes carved out by the spring runoff either.

Every time you move upstream you should do so with the feeling that you have covered all of the water in the section that you're leaving. Odds are you will have spent most of your casts working the banks, but it still pays to thoroughly cover the riffles and drift a few flies over slower-moving sections of the stream even if it looks like unproductive frog water.

All of the above tactics, with the exception of pulling a dry fly into the stream from the bank, can be employed with a dry fly and dropper fly. I'll admit that for the sake of simplicity and the pure joy of unweighted *single-fly* fly fishing, I do all I can to avoid droppers and even nymphing when it comes to wild meadow water. But I also recognize that I could catch more trout if I did employ some sort of dry fly/dropper system. So for those of you who may not be quite so

The actual line where the water depth changes is considered the sweet spot by most anglers when they fish a drop. PHOTO BY KYLE HENDRICKS

It's also important to fish the shallow riffle that occurs upstream of many drops. PHOTO BY KYLE HENDRICKS

The deeper water of the main channel is an obvious place to prospect for trout with a dry fly. PHOTO BY KYLE HENDRICKS

Once you cover the obvious water, make sure you also work the less obvious, more shallow riffles. PHOTO BY KYLE HENDRICKS

In some cases, the best trout may actually be feeding in the very shallow riffles that most fly fishers ignore.
PHOTO BY KYLE HENDRICKS

fastidious and for those days when you can't buy a strike on top, I recommend sticking to attractor-style weighted or beadhead nymph patterns such as the Gold-Ribbed Hare's Ear, Prince, Pheasant Tail, or Copper John.

The distance you put the dropper from the dry fly will depend somewhat on the depth of the water, but ten to fourteen inches is usually a good place to start. Remember too that the weighted dropper may hang up when you're working the shallower riffles. You might have to take it off or use an unweighted nymph imitation for some situations, but I try my hardest to not let it get that technical. I keep everything simple on purpose because what I enjoy the most is covering the water and reaching that wonderful meditative state that comes with walking, casting, and occasionally catching. There is concentration involved, but it's different from a day spent on the local spring creek fishing small flies to stubborn trout. And sometimes that in itself is a breath of fresh air.

If you've been around the fly-fishing block once or twice, you're probably thinking none of this stuff is new and that's true, although a little review never hurts. But what if the usual stuff doesn't work? It can happen. It might be as simple as the trout not feeding on top or your inability to draw them up to your hopper or attractor dry fly. Maybe you're on the water at an odd time of the year. It could be that you mistimed the runoff and the water is high and cooler than you'd like. It is a *wild* meadow stream, and like any other unregulated stream it has an annual cycle. There are a lot of reasons, but let's just say it's a day when you're having trouble figuring things out and you're not happy because this is unregulated, wild

water and it doesn't get that much pressure *and* you were the first fisherman through in the morning. You're thinking to yourself that it shouldn't be *that* hard to catch a trout.

I feel your pain. I was in a similar situation several years ago. I wasn't totally skunked, but let's just say the river wasn't acting the way I had come to expect it to behave. I wasn't having the gentle and restorative experience I was supposed to be having. And the hopper patterns that always worked that time of year weren't producing squat.

That's when I struck up a conversation with the only other fly fisher I'd seen on the water. He was quite a ways downstream from me when I first noticed him, but he was fishing fast toward me and he was catching fish along the way. When he got within earshot I asked the usual question and he said the fishing was great. Of course, that's when I asked the second usual question and he said, "Streamers." He then told me his story, and by the end of the day my go-to hopper patterns were sharing the "my favorite meadow water flies" distinction with streamers.

It turns out that the streamer fisherman was visiting Colorado from Wyoming, and he said it never crossed his mind to not fish my gentle, meandering meadow stream with streamers. He said it looked very similar to a number of the meadow streams he fished at home, and the fly pattern style of choice there was always streamers. He then showed me his setup. He was using a 9-foot moderately fast graphite rod tricked out with a medium density sink-tip fly line that had the tip portion cut back to just four feet. There was a stubby $3\frac{1}{2}$-foot-long section of 9-pound-test leader material nail knotted to it. He finished the rig off by

Larger meadow-stream trout are often most susceptible to streamer tactics.

using a loop knot to tie on a chunky size 4 black conehead Woolly Bugger streaked with blue Flashabou.

He fished the Woolly with a slightly down-and-across stream cast to the opposite bank, then stripped it a few times, wiggled the rod tip, and finally allowed the fly to swing downstream. When it was directly below him, he hesitated a moment and stripped it back. He then moved upstream several feet and repeated the process. I watched for the next twenty minutes as he methodically worked his way upstream, making just one cast and then moving, casting again and then moving. Occasionally, he slowed down enough to make two casts to the same spot, but then he continued upstream.

I was watching the fly line swing by a little point of grass that protruded into the current when the rod arced and a trout raced downstream. Several minutes later my jaw dropped when he guided a 3½-pound brown trout into the landing net. I'd fished that water for three seasons and never seen a trout anywhere close to that size!

He smiled and calmly said, "I'll bet there's more where he came from."

STREAMER BASICS FOR MEADOW WATER

Meadow water has never been the same for me since that day. I now see two streams where I used to see just one. There's the dry-fly water that I knew about and then there are the undercut banks, drop-offs to deep water, and subtle stream bank features that hide fewer, but often larger, trout that I didn't know about. It's almost like there are two layers of trout, and the techniques needed for one layer are totally different from those needed for the other.

Effective meadow-water streamer fishing requires an understanding of less obvious meadow-water structures, a willingness to cover a lot of water, knowledge of seasonal changes in unregulated meadow streams, and the use of standard and special tight-line streamer tactics.

Meadow-water streamer savvy begins with your fishing pace and direction of travel. You'll want to cover a lot of water. You can move more quickly if make your casts from the bank. Avoid wading wherever possible. If you do have to wade, remember that deposition zones in a meadow stream can be quite mucky—try to find gravel or hard-bottom areas when wading and get out of the stream and back up on the bank as soon as you can. Finally, pay attention to your footing when you are moving along the bank. Meadow stream banks are notoriously uneven and often have beaver or muskrat holes.

Unlike many tight-line fishing techniques, it's often best to work *upstream* when fishing meadow water because if you do have to wade, there is a good chance you'll muddy up the water. If conditions dictate that you fish downstream, it's even more important to wade as little as possible.

STREAMER TACTICS FOR MEADOW-WATER TROUT

The most commonly used meadow-water streamer tactic is the across-stream or across-and-downstream cast. You should try to get the fly as close to the opposite bank as possible. This is a standard tight-line tactic (see chapter 3) where an upstream mend will get the fly deeper or a downstream mend will

speed it up. You can shake out a few S curves of line after the cast if you want to delay the beginning of the swing. If a trout attacks the fly and misses, cast the fly back to the same swing line. There is always a chance that he'll whack it again.

It can be useful to fish a medium-density sink-tip line when you employ standard across-and-downstream tight-line tactics. Cut the sink-tip portion of the line back to just four or five feet for all but the largest meadow streams, or use an instant mini-sink tip that can be attached to your floating line with a loop-to-loop knot. The leader should be three to four feet long. Some anglers prefer to use a heavier pound test butt section and then a 1X or 0X tippet section, but an untapered section of 6- to 10-pound-test nylon or fluorocarbon will also get the job done.

Although a particular streamer fly pattern may be effective in some locales, it's usually adequate to carry several styles of light and dark patterns. Weighted patterns are best for all but the thinnest late-season water conditions. Some standards are Woolly Buggers, bunny-style patterns, and Muddlers. Pattern sizes should range from 2 to 6, although I carry some as large as size 2/0 for early-season, high, dirty water conditions and a few as small as size 8 for thin water.

There are several structural characteristics of meadow streams that you should pay special attention to. Undercut banks are the feature that most fly fishers associate with meadow water. Although undercut banks most often occur where the current cuts into an outside bank, they can also appear in some unusual places. That's one of the reasons why it's important to try to cover the

enough under the bank when you present it from the opposite side of the stream. If this happens, use a same-side downstream presentation.

To successfully execute a same-side downstream presentation, you must determine where the current first pushes into the undercut bank on your side of the river and then cast the fly downstream three or four feet out from that point. Once the fly has swung into the bank, immediately shake out some S curves of slack line to allow the current to pull the fly into the undercut. When the line tightens, slowly strip the fly back upstream as close to the bank as possible or better yet *under* the bank. You can accomplish this by holding the fly rod out over the water as you strip the fly back. When you get a strike, set the hook and immediately hold the rod as far out over the water as possible, tighten up on the fish, and then lever it out into open water to play it. It is important to not allow the trout to get back under the bank. Roots and debris are not uncommon where the river cuts under a bank, so don't be surprised if you occasionally lose a fish or snag your fly.

Another important holding area for meadow stream trout is on the inside of a bend. The water often cuts a deep hole where it enters the bend. Trout stack up in the soft water just off the drop and farther downstream on the inside of the bend. Always be sure to allow the fly to swing well over to the inside of the bend when you make an across-and-downstream presentation and then strip it back upstream.

Finally, pay attention to anything that protrudes into the current along the bank. It might be a clump of grass, a clod of dirt

It's usually adequate to carry several different pattern styles of weighted streamers in light and dark colors when tight lining for larger meadow stream trout.

opposite bank as thoroughly as possible when working your way upstream.

In most situations it's best to fish an undercut bank with a standard across-and-downstream presentation with a few strips and a wiggle or two. But there are situations where the current or an eddy won't allow the fly to sink down deep enough or get far

SAME-SIDE DOWNSTREAM PRESENTATION

Cast the fly a few feet out from where the current undercuts the bank, and then shake out S curves of slack once the current has pushed the fly into the bank.

The slack line helps the fly sink and allows it to be pushed under the bank.

Once the fly is right up alongside, or even under, the bank, strip it back.

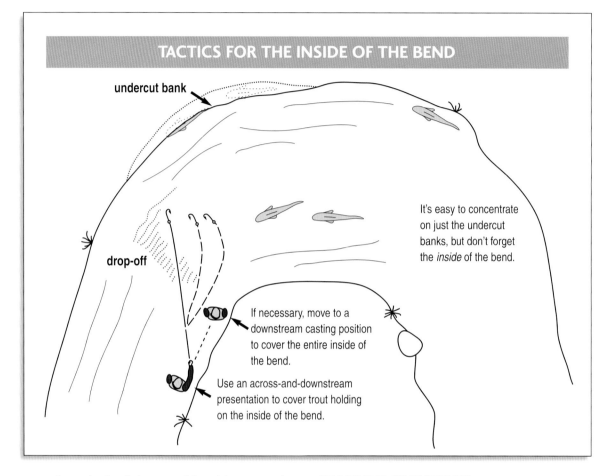

TACTICS FOR THE INSIDE OF THE BEND

undercut bank

drop-off

It's easy to concentrate on just the undercut banks, but don't forget the *inside* of the bend.

If necessary, move to a downstream casting position to cover the entire inside of the bend.

Use an across-and-downstream presentation to cover trout holding on the inside of the bend.

where the bank has caved in a bit, or a rock. The protrusion, no matter what size it is, will act as a velocity barrier and deflect the current. You may see these velocity barriers where the bank comes straight down into the water or where there is an undercut bank. It's an ideal holding area for trout.

An across-and-slightly downstream tight-line presentation is good for coaxing trout out from behind a protrusion. A perfect presentation swings the fly along or inside the current line created by the protrusion, but a trout will often attack the fly if you can just get it close. Remember to mend line upstream if the fly isn't sinking deep enough.

SEASONAL VARIATIONS

There are some important seasonal variations to consider when fishing unregulated meadow streams. My meadow-water streamer season often starts well before anyone else hits the water. I keep track of the flows during the spring runoff and try to fish the river right after the peak when the water begins to come down and clear up. These high flows are a prime time to catch larger meadow stream trout. The water is often discolored, but it isn't muddy, and it fills the entire stream channel. The increased flows and discoloration provide added cover for the larger fish that often feed with reckless aban-

A trout could be holding behind any of the inconspicuous bumps of grass that protrude into the stream on the outside of this bend.

don. It's best to use large, weighted streamers with two contrasting colors that show up well in the off-color water (see chapter 6). Typically the same meadow-water tight-line streamer fishing tactics that you use for normal water conditions will work during high water, but you might want to go to a stouter rod to handle the heavier current and the possibility of larger fish.

Late-season low-water conditions make streamer fishing more difficult. Try switching to a floating fly line with a 6- to 8-foot leader tapered to a 2X or 3X tippet. I usually start with a size 4 to 6 weighted streamer but will go to a smaller size in very clear, low-water situations if I'm not getting strikes. You can use the same meadow-water streamer tactics

that you would for normal flows when the water is low, but it's best to concentrate your efforts on the deep holes and undercut banks. If you don't think your fly is getting down deep enough in the holes, attach a split shot to the leader. Lighter color streamer patterns are often more effective in low, clear water, but you should always experiment with patterns that employ dark and light contrasting colors if you're not getting results with the light-colored flies. You'll probably have to cover even more water in the late season, but there is still a good chance of catching a larger-than-average trout. You'll increase your odds of low-water success by fishing in the early morning, evening, and on cloudy days when the light is low.

MEADOW STREAM MOUSING

Jackson Streit, the well known guide, outfitter, and guru of the upper South Platte River in South Park, and I were fishing one of his favorite sections of meadow water in South Park when he introduced me to his famous "strip, strip, wiggle, wiggle" streamer-fishing technique. The technique, which was actually a refinement of the Wyoming angler's idea of adding a little action to the fly after a strip, works best if you position yourself in an across-and-slightly-upstream position and cast the streamer as close as you can to the opposite bank. It's best to use a weighted streamer, short leader, and cutoff sink-tip line, and don't be scared to slap the fly down on the water. When the streamer hits, allow it to sink momentarily, and then in Jackson's words you "strip, strip, strip, wiggle, wiggle" as the fly swings down along the bank. The strips must be short and quick. The wiggle is accomplished by moving the rod tip back and forth over the water in a horizontal plane.

A deer-hair mouse pattern fished after dark imitates the field mice, voles, and pocket mice that are plentiful in the grassy environment around meadow streams.

The idea behind the strip and wiggle is that the strips entice the trout out from the undercut banks and the wiggle induces the strike. The wiggle actually allows the trout time to take a fast-moving streamer. It works like a charm and is another great technique to add to your toolbox.

Jackson opened another door for me on that trip when he nonchalantly asked if I'd ever fished meadow water on a full moon with a mouse pattern. He said that in years past he'd had a hoot casting deer-hair mousies after dark to the very water we were fishing and left it at that. Of course, he knew I'd be up there flailing around at the very next full moon—even if he was pulling my leg. But the reasoning did seem sound. The grassy environs that are so often associated with meadow water can be thick with the ultimate terrestrials—field mice, voles, and pocket mice. I'd seen them scooting through the grass when I was walking by the river. It only seemed logical that some of them would end up in the water, and if any larger trout were around, they'd eat them.

Although I'd tried night fishing with a fly rod a few times before, I can't say that the night-fishing bug ever really bit me, but I had managed to catch a few nice brown trout. But I figured that at least I wouldn't hang up my backcast so often if I was fishing meadow water. So I dutifully did my night-fishing homework: I staked out a few likely looking lies during the day and took the measure of the distances I would be casting and any muskrat holes I might stumble into in the middle of the night and waited for the full moon.

The full moon was already up when I got to the river, and my first surprise was how

No water is more beautiful than a stream meandering through grassland.

bright it was. I could actually see my shadow as I walked down to the river and was able to make out some details of the landscape. However, I did manage to stumble now and then until I got used to the weird attributes of moonlight, which pretty much shows everything in tones of gray. I'd already rigged up with a straight 6-foot section of 6-pound-test nylon tippet material on a 6-weight floating line before I left home. I carried a single spool of extra leader material and a few extra mouse patterns and that was it. I also made sure I had my headlamp with a red filter to protect my night vision, although I didn't need to use it on the walk in to the river.

The rest was pretty much just fishing. I tried casting the mouse across and upstream and across and downstream but eventually decided on the across-and-downstream presentation followed by a swing and waking retrieve. I was often able to see the fly when it hit the water, which was another surprise. I missed my first strike when a fish slashed at the fly and either missed it or I struck too quickly. It was another hour before I got another tug. I say tug because the trout very quietly took the fly as it slowly swung across the current. To be blunt, I was kind of spacing out and simply felt the line tighten up.

I think I managed to get the trout in fairly quickly, although most of what I remember is thinking that I must not allow it to get to the undercuts in the bank. I worked it pretty hard with the butt of the rod and managed to get a good look at a 23-

inch brown trout illuminated by the red light from my headlamp.

That trip led to several other full moon adventures that season and for several seasons afterwards. After that the fever died off a bit, but I still convince myself now and then that I should go. In the ensuing years, I have found that the trout seem to prefer the down-and-across presentation where I allow the fly to slowly swing and then periodically lift the rod tip to enhance its waking effect. Most of the time the takes are subtle, but occasionally a fish will blow up on the fly in a fashion similar to a largemouth bass. There have been some surprises too, such as the average-size or even smaller brown trout that are perfectly willing to attack the mouse and my discovery that the mouse patterns I tied with longer tails seem to work better than ones with shorter tails.

And finally, I should say this is work for a patient, meticulous angler. At least in my experience it has never been one fish after another, and there can be long lulls in the activity. But it is a hoot to be out after dark on a stream that you know in the daylight, if for no other reason than being outside at a weird time. And, of course, there have been a few memorable trout that keep me believing in the dream.

I came to meadow streams many years ago because I wanted to fool around with fishing hopper patterns, and on a more fundamental level I couldn't think of anything more beautiful than a stream meandering through grassland. I was never really out there to learn any secrets. But I have.

CHAPTER 5

Catching Difficult Trout

Taking the trout you want, the way you want

Among my fishing friends, A. K. Best comes closest to the concentration, precision, and patience of a heron. Right now we are on Colorado's Frying Pan River. A. K. is locked in on a trout rising in a long, oval eddy against the opposite bank. By anyone's standards, this would not be an easy fish. There is heavy water and the danger of a few overhanging tree branches between A. K. and the trout. These obstacles have forced him to stand upstream and across from the rising fish. Any other casting position would result in instant drag.

A. K. has cobbled together what looks like a downstream-and-across reach/slap cast that he underpowers to get the slack he needs to allow his fly to drift drag-free into the strike zone. The first couple casts have missed the drift line, but because he is close enough to the trout, he can raise the rod tip high and pick the dry fly off the water with

> The ancients wrote of the three ages of man; I propose to write of the three ages of the fisherman. When he wants to catch all the fish he can. When he strives to catch the largest fish. When he studies to catch the most difficult fish he can find, requiring the greatest skill and most refined tackle, caring more for the sport than the fish.
>
> EDWARD R. HEWITT
> *A Trout and Salmon Fisherman for Seventy-Five Years* (1948)

little or no disturbance. The trout doesn't spook. A. K. fine-tunes his casting position by moving a foot or so upstream, takes a moment to look at his fly and casts again, but it still isn't quite right. The process goes on another fifteen minutes before he settles into making near perfect casts that result in near perfect drifts over the trout.

87

A difficult-to-catch trout isn't always a large trout.

Ten minutes later, one of those presentations is apparently flawless. The trout tips up to the fly and sips it in. A. K.'s delighted laugh rings out across the valley. It's the laugh that over the years I've come to know means he's hooked up. I walk over to watch him land the trout. It's a chunky 11-inch brown trout.

"I know there are bigger fish, but that's the one I wanted!" A. K. sings out.

Defining what makes a trout difficult to catch isn't as easy as it sounds, but A. K.'s trout is a good place to begin. For many fly fishers, a difficult trout doesn't necessarily have to be a large trout. A. K.'s trout might very well have been a 20-incher—trout in difficult feeding lies are often larger because they are disturbed less and caught less. But in this case, the fish happened to be of modest size. Aside from size, the definition

of a difficult trout may have other, subtler characteristics that have more to do with the angler than the trout. I know that A. K. caught his trout on a size 20 quill body Blue-Winged Olive imitation of his own design. He shuns the increasingly popular practice of fishing a dry-fly dun imitation trailed by some sort of match-the-hatch emerger pattern. It doesn't matter to him that the two-fly setup may catch more trout. A. K. fishes the single dry fly because he doesn't like the way the two flies present on the water, and besides it just means more to him if he catches a trout on a single dry fly. Fly fishing has always been somewhat of a numbers and size-of-trout-caught game, but there are other meaningful goals and one of them is catching a trout the way you want to catch it. If this makes the fishing more difficult, that's fine because the potential rewards are so much greater.

But there is a hitch to the idea of catching trout the way you want to. Most of us have to earn the privilege with time spent on the water. Wayne Eng, the venerable Upper Sacramento and McCloud rivers fly-fishing guide and teacher, puts it nicely when he says that "difficult trout are most often caught by design, rather than luck." To catch a trout by design implies that you must have tackle that is suited to the conditions, skill in using that tackle, knowledge of the trout, and finally an understanding of the river itself. You may be able to speed up the process with study and some competent instruction, but it will still take time. If you decide to do the work, you will ultimately find yourself in a position where you really do understand what it means to catch a trout the way you want to catch it. And be forewarned: This will happen about the time you realize that your definition of what makes a trout difficult to catch is going to change over time.

TACTICS FOR DIFFICULT TROUT

With those mysteries in mind, let's consider some of the hard-core tactical realities of catching difficult trout. Although every difficult trout that you encounter will come with its own unique challenges, the odds are that you will find many of these fish difficult because they are selectively feeding or positioned in difficult lies. The more tricks you have in your bag for solving the underlying reasons that make a trout difficult to catch, the better able you'll be to put together the combinations of tactics that will be required to catch the most difficult of trout.

Selective Feeders

American fly fishermen spend a lot of time trying to match what the trout are eating. Groundbreaking books such as Ernest Schwiebert's *Matching the Hatch* (1955) and Doug Swisher and Carl Richards's *Selective Trout* (1971) form the basis for the way fly fishing is taught in the United States. And there's no question that fly fishermen who pay attention to the size, color, and silhouette of the foods that trout are eating and then match them fairly closely with an artificial fly have higher success rates.

Fly fishers intent on catching difficult trout need to integrate match-the-hatch principles into a broader working model that includes matching fly patterns to trout riseforms and matching key elements of the hatch as it progresses.

The first step toward a broader working model is to consider any hatch as a

Although you may see a few trout rising, the majority of the trout may still be feeding below the surface. This is especially true at the beginning of the hatch.

continuum where the numbers of insects in various stages of emergence are constantly changing. Consider that at the beginning of the hatch the bulk of insects will be emerging nymphs or pupae. As the hatch progresses, more and more of the insects will be adults. In general, trout are opportunists, and you can expect that they'll feed on the most abundant or easiest to catch source of insects. That means at the beginning of the hatch they'll be taking nymphs and pupae below the surface. As the hatch progresses, they'll usually switch over to duns in the case of mayflies, but this may not necessarily be true for the harder to catch caddisfly or midge adults. If the caddisflies or midges are getting

A headless head-to-tail rise can mislead anglers into believing that the majority of feeding is taking place on the surface when it's actually still occurring below the surface. ILLUSTRATED BY DEBRA ROSE

The head-to-tail rise indicates that the trout are feeding on insects in the surface film or occasionally on newly hatched adults. The key is to watch the newly hatched adults on the surface and see if the trout are consistently taking them. ILLUSTRATED BY DEBRA ROSE

Fly patterns that sit down in the surface film are best for most difficult trout situations. Try to have a variety of pattern styles such as (from left) hairwing Comparadun, parachute with a dubbed body, parachute with a quill body, and CDC Comparadun. Traditionally hackled patterns (far right) are often less effective on difficult trout, but may save the day in faster-moving water or as an imitation of duns that are rapidly getting into the air.

If you get refusal rises, try using the same fly pattern one size smaller.

off the surface and quickly into the air, the trout might spend a little more time vacuuming up the easier to catch but less abundant pupae.

Trout often become difficult to catch when the nymph-to-dun ratio is close to equal. This occurs at the front end of a mayfly hatch when the first of the duns appear on the water's surface. Fly fishers who switch over to a dry-fly pattern as soon as they see the duns often have a difficult time. The trout's riseform is the key to understanding why these anglers have difficulties.

Typically the fish will be making what I call headless head-to-tail rises or porpoising

riseforms where you see the trout's back, dorsal fin, and tail. This is a surefire sign that they are still feeding on emerging nymphs just under the surface. If you match your fly pattern to the riseform, you'll be using a wet fly, soft-hackle nymph, or even an unweighted nymph fished just below the surface. Don't let the duns on the surface fool you until you actually observe a significant number of them being taken by the trout.

If you watch closely, you'll spot another riseform change before the more complete switchover to the duns. This is the head-to-tail rise where you actually see the trout's head come out of the water. It means the prey is right in the surface film, and you can match the riseform with a floating nymph, greased wet fly, or soft-hackle fly.

Theory aside, the practical aspect of all this is that you must constantly evaluate the situation when rising trout are difficult to catch. Make sure that your artificial matches the location in the water column where the action is taking place. Use the riseforms to help you. A currently popular tactic is to trail a nymph, soft-hackle-style wet fly, or floating nymph anywhere from a foot to two feet behind a dun or adult imitation during the hatch transitions. At the front end of the hatch, the two-fly rig covers you for the occasional trout that hits the dun and helps suspend a nymph or soft-hackle in the strike zone just below the surface. As the hatch progresses, you may be able to take the trailer off and fish a single dry fly.

Remember that when it comes to difficult trout it may be just as important to put the fly where the trout is expecting to see it as it is to have the perfect match. I can remember any number of times during difficult hatches where I may not have had the perfect fly, but I was able to figure out where the heaviest feeding was taking place. The trout took my imperfect match because it was where they expected the food to be.

I use some other tricks when feeding selectivity makes catching trout difficult. If you get a refusal rise, switch to the same fly pattern style in a smaller size. Use dry-fly pattern types that sit down in the surface film, and carry a variety of different styles such as parachutes, Comparaduns, no-hackles, or CDCs. You may find that the trout will favor one style over another or that they may prefer one style at the beginning of the hatch and another toward the end. Always have examples of each pattern type with a trailing shuck.

Another special feeding behavior that makes trout difficult to catch occurs regularly on a river not far from where I live. I can't put an exact date on the calendar, but I can pretty much figure that it will occur between the middle of June and the middle of July. Any more precision is impossible due to the vagaries of runoff, weather, and the trout themselves, but I can say that the wild irises are usually in bloom when it happens.

Multiple Hatches

During those special few weeks, I look for size 16 tan caddisflies, female Trico duns, male and female spent Trico spinners, Yellow Sallies, Pale Morning Duns, a smaller dark female caddisfly that dives, a smattering of tiny chartreuse midges, and, at least early on, a few Blue-Winged Olives to all make an appearance on the water before noon. It is a vision that has shepherded me through many a cold winter's night.

Of course, this event is the storied complex hatch. Some writers have gotten more mysterious by calling it a masking hatch when the trout appear to be taking one insect when in fact they are taking something else. I once heard a fly shop owner say that the guides call it a complex hatch because they don't have a clue what the trout are taking! I keep it simple by just calling it a multiple hatch. Needless to say, the challenge of any multiple hatch is first figuring out what the trout are really taking and then being aware of the possibility that they may switch to another hatching, diving, or spent insect at any time. The switch is often

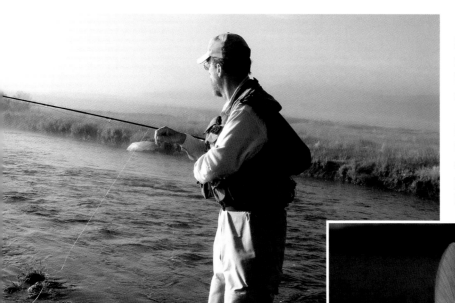

Female Tricos often hatch early in the morning. When they do, it pays to be on the river.
PHOTO BY JANA RUSH

Female Tricos are the first of a number of aquatic insects that can play a role in a multiple hatch.

subtle, and at the beginning it isn't necessarily telegraphed by the presence of large numbers of the newly favored insect on the surface.

The insect diversity of the multiple hatch that occurs on my river makes it a good teaching tool for a discussion on how to determine when the trout's feeding preference changes and what fly patterns and tactics to use when it does. From the start, it's important to understand that there is often more than one solution to catching trout during a multiple hatch. Sometimes all it takes is a good presentation of the same fly pattern that was working before you noticed that the trout switched their feeding preference. This occurs because there may still be a few fish

who will take the imitation even though the thrust of the feeding has switched elsewhere. Having said that, though, I can also say that there will be other times when the trout will unequivocally switch from one insect to another, and if you fail to recognize the change in feeding, you will stop getting strikes.

So as an example, here is the chronology of my favorite multiple hatch and what I do during its various stages.

I start off by getting to the river early because the female Trico duns hatch within an hour or so of first light. This won't always be necessary for this particular single hatch. It will go through a number of transformations as it continues for the next three months, but during the few weeks of the multiple hatch

The classic ringed riseform indicates the trout are feeding on hatching female Tricos.

it pays to watch things develop from the very start. Besides, getting on the water early gives me a shot at catching a fish or two before things get complicated with multiple hatches. Also, the trout are often a little more forgiving first thing in the morning when they are hungry and there's just a smattering of Trico duns on the water's surface. They'll be a lot pickier a few hours later when spent spinners are everywhere and caddisflies and Pale Morning Duns are popping.

Once the hatch begins, the first thing to be aware of are the riseforms. The rise to a dun typically leaves the classic ring on the water's surface. You might even see a trout or two turn and chase an emerging dun for a short distance. This riseform is important to note because you will see a definite switch when the trout begin taking spent spinners in a few hours. Observing the riseforms and certain feeding behaviors are the key to determining when the trout switch their feeding preference. The other key observation you'll have to make is whether there are any other insects in the air or on the water.

When the Trico duns are hatching, it is not uncommon to also see a sparse caddisfly hatch. There are never a lot of them, but they're important, and you can be sure the trout know about them. If I see two or three caddis on or over the water during the dun hatch, that's all it takes for me to switch over to a two-fly rig. I usually tie on an Elk Hair Caddis of the appropriate size and trail my Trico dun imitation a foot and a half or so behind it.

Although there may be only a few caddis in the air, it is surprising how often the trout take the caddis imitation! And believe me, this won't be the first time during this multiple hatch that you'll see the trout switch from a more plentiful food source to one that is scarcer. The point is that when you're dealing with a multiple hatch always be aware when there are other insects on the water, and if necessary experiment with imitations of those insects no matter how few there are.

As the dun hatch progresses, the trout will continue to occasionally smash the caddisfly imitation even though more and more duns are on the water. Eventually the dun hatch will peter out, followed by a period of relative calm. It's possible to pick up a fish or two either on the dun imitation or the caddis during this period, but it's also not a bad idea to rest the water. On the sweetest days, you will find that the feeding activity on the duns segues smoothly into the spinnerfall without pause.

It's not always obvious that the spent spinners are even on the water. They are hard to see, and the mating swarm may have fallen a bit farther upstream out of view. The one sure sign that the trout are off the duns is the riseforms. Look for a more subtle head rise that's almost like a sip. As more and more spinners end up on the water, you may witness somewhat more frantic head rises as the trout try to chow down on as many spinners as possible. You may see fish methodically feeding upstream for several feet or more and then drift back downstream and do it all over. Others may casually sway a few inches from side to side to pick off the spinners.

A massive mating swarm of Tricos over the water's surface signals that the spinnerfall is imminent, but it may not be visible if it occurs upstream.

This Trico spinnerfall and the feeding activity it creates is like the base paint an artist applies to the canvas before he begins work. All the other hatches are embedded in it.

There are two approaches to fishing the spinnerfall itself. First you can fish a single Trico spinner imitation. Standard dry-fly tactics apply here. Try one pattern for a while, and if it doesn't work, switch to another

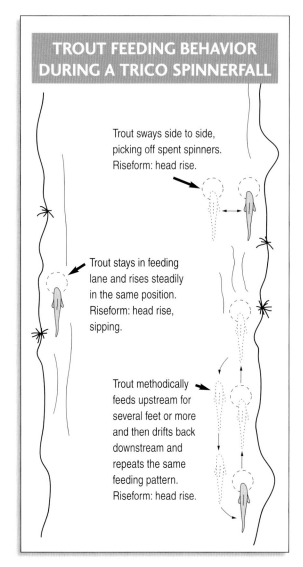

TROUT FEEDING BEHAVIOR DURING A TRICO SPINNERFALL

Trout sways side to side, picking off spent spinners. Riseform: head rise.

Trout stays in feeding lane and rises steadily in the same position. Riseform: head rise, sipping.

Trout methodically feeds upstream for several feet or more and then drifts back downstream and repeats the same feeding pattern. Riseform: head rise.

The other approach is to leave the Elk Hair Caddis imitation on and trail the spinner pattern behind it. This is an old guide trick to help a less experienced client see where the tiny, difficult-to-see Trico spinner is on the water. The Elk Hair Caddis also acts as a strike indicator if you fail to see the fish take the spinner imitation. In a multiple hatch situation where the trout are aware that there are also caddis hatching, you may even find that you get more hookups on the caddis than the spinner. Of course, you may also find that the caddis imitation puts the trout down and you'll be forced to use a single spent spinner imitation or at least a smaller size dry fly in the two-fly rig.

Here comes the part that many anglers miss. Let's say there are trout rising everywhere to the spent spinners, and it's all you can do to just stay on task and make casts to the more consistent risers. Life is good. You're getting a few strikes and even landing some trout on the tiny spinners and 6X tippet. As the spinnerfall continues, you notice that you're not getting as many strikes as you did earlier, but that's okay because you figure there are more spinners on the water and maybe the trout are beginning to fill up. It isn't okay when forty-five minutes go by and you realize the trout haven't even given your fly a look.

That's when you decide to take a break. You're staring out at the water when you notice that some of the fish are behaving differently than those that are rising to the spent spinners. These trout are darting a foot or so from side to side and feeding with more authority. This isn't the lackadaisical sashaying here and there to take a spent spinner that isn't going anywhere. These trout are

pattern style of the same fly. If I get a single refusal rise to the artificial, I immediately switch to another pattern style. My philosophy is that most Trico spinnerfalls occur on relatively slow-moving water where the trout can get a pretty good look at the fly. I figure if it isn't dragging and I get a refusal, I'll keep getting refusals, so I switch the fly right away.

On any given day, trout may show a preference for a particular spent spinner fly pattern, so it pays to have a variety of pattern styles.

on the hunt. That's when you notice a single Pale Morning Dun zipping through the air. You wonder, "Could it be?" and decide to switch to a Pale Morning Dun imitation. The first cast proves that the trout are interested in the PMD for sure, but you get a refusal rise. You realize you're on to something, but maybe the fly was dragging, so you cast again. You get another refusal rise, and when you try the presentation on a different fish in a different lie you still get a refusal.

Panic hasn't exactly set in because you figure you still might be able to catch a few dummies on the Trico spinner imitation, but it would be nice to figure out what was going on. That's when you decide to trail a floating nymph imitation of the PMD behind the dun imitation. It can't hurt. As soon

The head rise is a surefire indication that the trout are taking spent Trico spinners whether the mating swarm is visible or not.

An aggressive riseform—such as this to an emerging Pale Morning Dun—that occurs when trout are taking spent spinners almost always heralds the entrance of another insect species to the multiple hatch mix.

as the flies hit the water a trout races over and gobbles up the floating nymph. You land and release it, and on the next cast the same thing happens. In fact, wherever you cast the floating nymph a trout chooses it over the more plentiful spent spinners every time. It's a beautiful thing, but it's over in a half hour.

Before you're even done reminiscing about how great the fishing was and how you figured out the multiple hatch, the air fills with small black caddisflies. You notice that your waders are covered in them *below* the waterline. It's immediately apparent that things are changing again, but you can't verify it by observing any changes in the number or type of riseforms. You decide to switch anyway to a diving caddis imitation trailed behind an Elk Hair Caddis. The anticipation is incredible, but after a half hour you don't get a single strike to the diving caddis pattern, although you do pick up a trout on the caddis.

You switch back to a spinner trailed behind the caddis and pick up a few more trout before things begin to peter out. When it all settles out you sit down on the bank and scratch your head. What a ride. You wonder if the trout ignored the diving caddis or if you just didn't fish it right or if the four or five Yellow Sallies you saw chugging through the mating swarms of Tricos could have also meant something.

That's pretty much the way it goes with multiple hatches. So how do you apply my multiple hatch lessons to your home waters? First pay attention to riseforms. Any change in the rising behavior of the trout almost always means a change in what they're feeding on. When riseforms change, take some time to observe the air and the water's surface for different species or life stages of insects. If a new insect species does appear on the scene, imitate it no matter how few you see. You can still use the pattern that has been productive by employing a two-fly rig with the imitation of the newly observed insect as a trailer.

Finally, pay attention to any change in feeding behavior. If the trout change from casual or lackadaisical behavior to more active behavior, you can almost bet that they have switched to feeding on a different insect species. If you don't see anything in the air, sample the drift. Once you've determined what the new insect is, experiment with imitations of its various life phases until you get results. If a dun imitation doesn't work, try trailing a floating nymph or beadhead nymph or a cripple or even a spent spinner!

The key is to recognize when the productive pattern that you've been using seems to become less effective but the trout continue rising. If there are different species of insects in the air or on the water, you might be in a multiple hatch situation. If you can crack the mystery of what insect the trout have switched to and then successfully present an imitation of that insect where you need to, get ready for a very good day on the river.

Trout in Difficult Lies

Presentation is the key to catching trout in difficult lies. Your definition of presentation should include how you approach the trout, your casting position, and finally the cast. Most fly fishers understand that difficult trout should be approached in a way that won't disturb them. You need to keep the sun at your back and, if possible, don't wade at all. If you must wade, be slow, careful, and quiet. The old standard rule of approaching the fish from downstream is good advice, but

modern tactics for difficult fish may require you to get into an upstream or upstream-and-across casting position. If you must approach from upstream, it's more likely that the trout will detect you, so keep your distance and be stealthy.

Next to the cast itself, your casting position is the most crucial. Get as close to the fish as possible. Conditions and experience will dictate how close that is. Good casting position translates directly to drag-free drift. The closer you can get to the fish, the less line you'll have on the water. Less line on the water always makes it easier to control drag. So do yourself a favor and get as close as you can whenever the opportunity presents itself because you can be sure there will be plenty of times when you'll have to lengthen your cast to make up for a less than advantageous casting position.

Traditionally, fly fishermen cast straight upstream to rising trout.

Most guides will tell you that the most common fly-fishing deficiency they see is casting ability. This is especially true when it comes to fishing casts that help neutralize drag. Fishing casts require practice, and whether you spend time casting on the lawn or on the river, it really does pay to put the time in. If you want to catch difficult trout, you'll need expertise in parachute, reach, check, and S curve casts. With these casts or combinations of them, you'll be able to cover most of the difficult trout situations.

Tackle refinements may be necessary for some situations, but in general seek out the longest length fly rod you can get away with and one that has an action that you feel comfortable casting. The rod won't make you more accurate, but if you don't have to concentrate on making it cast right, you'll be able to concentrate on accuracy. Leader length will ultimately be determined by conditions, but try to come up with a standard length leader for the conditions where you most typically fish. You'll find that your casts will be a lot more accurate if you use the same length leader as much as possible. You might also consider tying a few leaders with a hard nylon butt section (I like Maxima Chameleon) and soft nylon for the midsection and tippet. I've found that leaders of this composition, no matter what the formula is, tend to naturally land with S curves in the tippet.

With experience, you'll learn which fishing casts apply to the most common difficult lies. A trout that's rising in the slower water along the opposite bank where the faster water of the main channel is between you and the fish is a common problem. Depending on the speed of the fast water between you and the fish, you might be able to pile

The reach cast is the only cast where the rod finishes in an upstream position, which allows you to follow the fly's downstream drift with the rod tip and results in longer drag-free drifts.

Lower the rod parallel to the water during the delivery stroke of the parachute (also called the puddle or pile) cast. This reduces the line speed, causing the fly line to land on the water first.

When the leader lands on the water, it forms a series of drag-defeating S curves.

The check, or stop, cast is executed by stopping the rod abruptly on the power stroke and not shooting line.

When the line bounces back, it falls to the water in a series of S curves. PHOTOS BY ANGUS DRUMMOND

up enough tippet with a parachute cast to get the job done. But the ultimate cast in this situation is a downstream-and-across reach cast, which is nothing more than an aerial mend (an on-water mend is seldom useful for difficult fish). The great advantage of this cast is that you finish the cast with the rod tip *upstream*. That means you can follow the drift downstream with the rod tip and get a few more seconds of drag-free drift! Throwing a few S curves into the reach cast may buy you a few more seconds.

A trout rising within inches of the bank may require that you underpower a cast onto the bank and gently pull the fly into the water. A downstream-and-across reach cast executed under the same conditions may allow you a bit longer drift because

when you pull the fly into the water you'll be able to follow its downstream drift with the rod tip.

Subsurface feeding trout become difficult when it's hard to get a drag-free drift to them or when they are feeding in thin water. If you are having difficulty getting the drift right, sometimes all it takes is moving your casting position a foot or two upstream, downstream, or closer to or farther from the fish. Never underestimate the power of moving just a little bit to reduce drag, whether you are nymphing or fishing dry flies!

Nymphing to trout feeding in thin water may require that you remove the strike indicator and any weight that you may have attached to the leader. If possible, try to get as close to the trout as you can and use

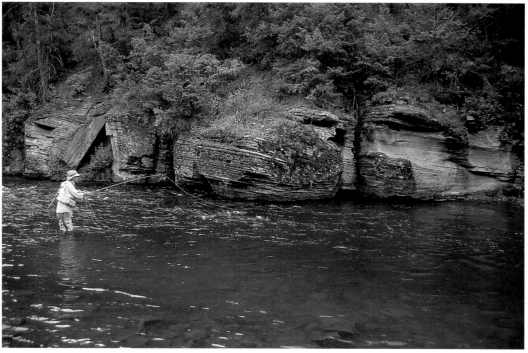

A downstream-and-across reach cast is ideal when a trout is rising along the opposite bank and a tongue of faster current is between you and the trout.

You may not need to cast a dry fly 3 or 4 feet upstream from a steadily rising trout. Try casting the fly just a foot or so upstream of the fish. The shortened drift may be less affected by micro-drag.

short-line nymphing tactics to hold the fly line completely off the water. Finally, watch the trout to see when it takes your imitation. There is no better strike indicator.

Another trick for trout in difficult lies is to use the riseform disturbances on the water's surface to cover your leader on smooth, thin water. Finally, let's say you're fishing to some steady risers that aren't moving around much, and changing your casting position a foot or two this way or that doesn't work. It might be time to try another micro-adjustment. Rather than casting the fly three or four feet upstream of the targeted fish, try putting it just a foot or so above it. Sometimes the *shorter* the drift the less there is that can go wrong, especially when it comes to micro-drag.

The time will come when you encounter the ultimate double whammy—a selective feeder in a difficult lie. In this situation, it always pays to try to make your first cast your best cast because a good first cast gives you the greatest chance for success. But before you make that cast it's important to position yourself where you can recover the fly without spooking the trout if the cast is off target or if the trout simply doesn't take it. Remember, a selectively feeding trout in a difficult lie is about as tough as a difficult trout situation can get. You're going to need to present the right fly with the right cast to where the trout is looking for it. It may sound like hocus-pocus, but that most important first cast may come off better if you take a few moments to visualize exactly where you want the fly to go *and* how you're going to respond if the trout takes it. And most important, you're going to have to really believe that you can catch that trout and not walk past it to an easier fish.

You may not fare well on that first truly difficult trout that you go after, but sooner or later there will be a single selectively rising trout in a seemingly impossible lie that, against all odds, you decide to give a try. It will be the kind of trout that you never in your wildest dreams figured you could catch. You'll take the time to figure out the best casting position, and you'll make your first cast count. And then you'll watch the trout tip up and take your fly exactly the way it took the natural that drifted over it a few minutes before.

That's when you'll understand what Hewitt was talking about when he wrote about the third and final age of a fisherman.

CHAPTER 6

High-Water Strategies

Spring and storm runoffs, off-color and dirty water

It usually doesn't really feel like springtime in the Rockies until the month of June, which also means that somewhere in Colorado there will be a river, stream, or brook that is swelled with snowmelt. This isn't always good news, especially since most of us have been primed for dry flies by the Blue-Winged Olive hatch that can begin anytime from late February on. And actually, if you don't mind a bit of a chill, you could be getting primed for the Olives by fishing to some pretty good midge hatches anywhere from January on.

I've seen the spring runoff create some major personality changes in my fly-fishing pals. Some of them sink into depression or a manic cycle of no fishing but lots of fly tying. Others cross the line and play golf for the next month or participate in one of the other dark sports that I don't know how to play. Most report to the nearest tailwater and

hope that the runoff isn't so severe that the local water board is forced to increase the flows to unfishable levels. Worse yet, there's always the chance that the flows will be so high that the runoff actually pours over the dam's spillway.

And then there are fishermen like me who may forget about the runoff altogether or somehow think that it doesn't apply to them and head to their favorite stream only to find that it looks like chocolate milk or worse. For many years I just went home when that happened or diverted to the nearest tailwater. That was before gasoline got so expensive and before it occurred to me that maybe I should just take some time and see if I might be able to catch a trout anyway.

I'll be the first to admit that I'd rather be putting the sneak on a trout that's finning the clear water of a sweet little mountain brook, but what are you going to do? I'm a

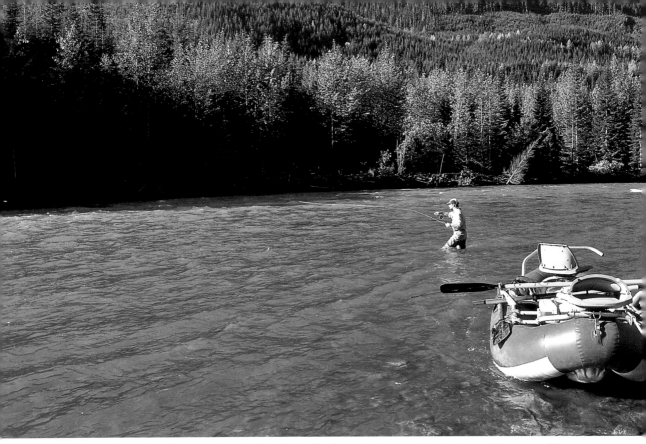

Most fly fishers have less experience fishing high, off-color water because they try to avoid those conditions whenever possible.

12-month-a-year fly fisherman, so for me that has meant forcing myself to learn something about catching trout during high-water conditions. High water might mean the spring runoff, a big water release from the local tailwater, or the high flows resulting from a summer thunderstorm. And I should say I still have to sometimes force myself to fish high water because it's never very easy.

There are several reasons why this is true. First, most of us don't get or take the opportunity to fish high water as much as we fish more normal flows. And even if you do take the challenge and learn a few high-water tricks, the chances are good that you still won't catch as many trout as you might dur-

ing more normal flows. It could be that the trout simply shut down when the flows are high because it's the spring runoff and the snowmelt has chilled the water to the point that their metabolism and appetite slows. Another possibility is that the high water has spread the fish out all over the river and you can't find them, or the water is dirty enough that the trout can't find the fly you're trying to show them. It may even be that the high water has supersaturated the water column with so much food that the trout have eaten their fill and can't be tempted with artificial flies. Or maybe the high flows have kicked a food source into the river that's only available during runoff, and you've never even seen or thought about imitating it.

All of this means that you're going to have to make some changes if you want to catch fish, and the first one should be your mindset. You can't start off thinking the day's fishing is hopeless just because the water is high. I tell myself that the fishing might very well be difficult, but the trout still have to eat. If I can get a fly in front of them, a strike is possible. I also make sure to remind myself that although I may know a river like the back of my hand at lower water flows, when it's high it's a brand new river, and I need to start from scratch. The trout *aren't* going to be where I'm used to finding them, and the first step to high-water success is figuring out where they are and how active they are.

CHARACTERISTICS OF EARLY-SEASON SNOWMELT

A good place to start is with water clarity. Most fly fishermen would rather deal with high, relatively clear water than high, roily, or muddy water. But you may want to reconsider that. Where I live in the Rockies, some streams will run high and clear right at the onset of spring runoff. The clear water may last a week or so before it begins to dirty. At this time, it's easy to think you have a pretty good shot at finding and catching a few trout. That's especially true if you've ever fished the similar-looking high, clear water that occurs at the *end* of the runoff cycle when most of the mud has washed out of a stream but the water volume is still high.

All I can say is don't get your hopes up. I've found that the high, clear water at the beginning of the runoff cycle is often the initial snowmelt from the top of the snowpack. The reason it's clear is because the ground beneath may still be frozen. The

good news is that the water is clear, but the bad news is that this first pulse of snowmelt significantly lowers the stream's water temperature. If you know what the stream's pre-runoff flows look like, figure that the greater the volume of snowmelt in it, the lower the water temperature is going to be. And that low water temperature can significantly lower a trout's metabolism, which will dampen its appetite.

There are a few things you can do to overcome early-season, cold-water temperatures. Target side channels, backwaters, sections of the stream that receive the most sun, and places where the current is slow and the water is shallow. These water types provide the conditions that may allow the water to heat up the extra few degrees that are needed to kick in the trout's feeding instincts. Also be on the lookout for any springs that may enter the stream. Spring water is warmer than the snowmelt-cooled stream water, and trout will gather there to feed. Finally, assume you will probably have to fish subsurface fly patterns, and no matter what fly you choose to use, make a point to fish it as slow as possible. In most cases, this means a using a weighted pattern that you can dead-drift along the stream bottom.

I'm not picky about fly patterns when I'm fishing the clear, super-cooled waters of the early-season runoff because I've found that it's more important to just get a fly in front of the trout and keep it there as long as I can. For the most part, my go-to fly is a substantially weighted Prince Nymph. By substantial I mean lead wire or a nontoxic equivalent wrapped around the shank *and* a tungsten bead. I like the fly in a size 10 or 12 for the waters I fish, and sometimes I'll trail a smaller size 14 to size 18 Brassie or Copper John behind it for effect. Although I occasionally fish a larger weighted streamer just to see what will happen, I almost always do better with the smaller nymphs. If you do decide to try a streamer in these conditions, I recommend high-sticking something that is heavily weighted.

The consolation to the often predictably slow fishing during the initial icy-cold runoff is that you can figure the water temperatures will usually moderate significantly in just a week or so, and that in itself can be enough to jump-start feeding activity. Of course, the downside is that along with the warmer water temperatures you can expect off-color water. Needless to say, off-color water can mean anything from an earthy tint to a soupy chocolate milk.

OFF-COLOR WATER

When the water is off-color, I figure it's a good sign if I can see my wading shoes when I'm standing in two feet of water. If my feet disappear in a foot or less water, I consider it to be muddy. When I encounter dirty water conditions, the first thing I check out is whether the entire river is discolored or if one side is noticeably more turbid than the other. If just one side is muddy, I fish my way up the clearer side first, paying special attention to the area within three or four feet of the bank and where any clear tributaries come in.

Although I've heard and read about how much trout like to hang on the mud line between the dirty and clear water, in practice I've often found just as many fish close in to the bank on the clear-water side. This

By all means explore the line between muddy and clear water, but don't forget to fish nearby clear water, too.

Wind-generated mud lines on lakes can provide productive fishing, but a mud line in a river is often a different story.

doesn't mean you shouldn't explore the mud line with both nymph and streamer patterns and that you won't catch fish there. Just don't let the mud line seduce you into not thoroughly covering the clear-water side of the river *before* you wade out to fish it. Also, I've noticed that when I do catch fish from the mud line it's almost always the result of casting a streamer into the muddy water from the clear-water side and swinging or stripping it back out into the clear water.

Finally, I should note that my inconsistent mud line success on moving waters differs considerably from the experiences I've had fishing the wind-generated mud lines on lakes and reservoirs where I've caught numerous large trout working the mud.

When you encounter water that is dirty on just one side of the stream, you will

High, off-color water presents a separate set of challenges that are often difficult, but it's not impossible to catch a trout.

sometimes find that a tributary or some other disturbance such as a bridge repair is causing the discoloration. So if you have qualms about fishing the dirty stuff, you might consider hiking or driving upstream a way to see if you can locate the source of the discoloration, and simply begin your fishing above it.

If a stream is experiencing full-blown spring runoff, you're probably not going to find a point source of discoloration, such as a muddied tributary, unless you are fishing a tailwater or spring creek. The odds are that once the runoff begins, whether it's a small stream or a larger river, you're going to be dealing with high, off-color or muddy water. Although I use basically the same tactics when fishing high, off-color water as I do for muddier high water, if given the choice, I'll always fish the off-color water simply because it just *looks* like I'll have a better chance of success.

Tactics for Off-Color Water

The most important thing to remember about high, off-color water is that the trout probably don't like it much better than you do. They will seek out slower-moving water near the banks, in backwaters, along the inside of bends, behind rocks, in side channels, and along the stream bottom where the water velocity is slowed by the friction between the rocky streambed and the water.

When I first decided to try to find ways to catch trout during the runoff, I relied almost solely on short-line, dead-drift nymphing tactics. I found that I could effectively work the slower water near the banks by simply standing on the bank and methodically dead-drifting nymph patterns on a short line.

At first I used the same match-the-hatch fly patterns that I used when the river was at lower levels. Later I started experimenting with larger attractor-style nymphs such as beadhead Gold-Ribbed Hare's Ears, Princes, and Copper Johns. My reasoning was that the larger fly would be more visible to the trout and that they might be more inclined to attack a larger meal. It eventually occurred to me that just because the water is off-color it doesn't mean that you can't match what you find in the drift. That's when I started seining the river close in to the bank wherever I was fishing. In addition to the aquatic insect nymphs and pupae that I was used to seeing in the river during non-runoff times, I also found aquatic worms, earthworms, larger stonefly nymphs, crane fly larvae, dead baitfish, unidentified grubs, a surprising number of beetles and other terrestrials, cased caddis larvae, and scuds. There was also a fair amount of inanimate stuff such as twigs, smaller pieces of wood, algae, shredded aquatic and terrestrial plants, and some human-related trash such as strike indicators, cigarette butts, and discarded paper.

My drift sampling made me curious about what the trout actually were eating, so when I did manage to catch one on my Prince or Hare's Ear, I took stomach samples. The contents were pretty much what you would figure. There were a lot of earthworms (the brown trout seem to especially like them) and aquatic worms. Where crane fly larvae were available, I found that the trout did eat them, but not in the numbers that I thought they might based on availability. I also occasionally found some pretty mutilated baitfish, which I took to be either dead or crippled when they were eaten. It

High, off-color water forces the trout in toward the slower-moving water near the banks, behind rocks, and into less turbulent backwaters. The left side of the river pictured here is a good example of these criteria and may very well hold trout.

was interesting to note that it wasn't just the larger fish that took the baitfish. Smaller trout also gobbled down the baitfish, which I took as a further sign that they might already be dead or crippled and were an easy-to-catch target of opportunity. Other items of interest were some large beetles that appeared more often than I would have thought and a surprising number of fish with gobs of algae in their stomachs or even little bits of wood.

The stomach samples led me to the conclusion that I hadn't been too far off using my larger, heavily weighted, general-purpose, attractor-nymph patterns. As a rule, the darker patterns with broader silhouettes

High water levels may kick scuds or aquatic worms that aren't normally available to the trout into the drift.

Larger, weighted versions of standard go-to nymph patterns such as (from left) the Pheasant Tail, Gold-Ribbed Hare's Ear, and Prince Nymph are a good place to start when fishing high, off-color water.

A size 10 conehead Gold-Ribbed Hare's Ear is an excellent choice to anchor a two-fly nymphing rig when the water is high and off-color.

seemed to work the best, although brighter wire-style patterns along the lines of a Copper John were a pretty close second. It made sense to me that on brighter days the darker patterns would show up better in the off-color water, but I didn't have any real proof. It also made sense that a fly with a broader profile would be easier for the trout to pick out. The fact that some of the fish had eaten inanimate junk also indicated that they occasionally made mistakes when feeding, either because they couldn't see the object well or it was moving too quickly and they just snapped it up on instinct. Whatever the reason, a large, dark beadhead Hare's Ear could cover a lot of ground imitating natu-rals as well as the occasional bit of inanimate debris that might fool a trout into feeding.

Eventually I experimented with two-fly rigs. For general-purpose, off-color, high water, I'd start with a size 10 weighted bead-head Prince or beadhead Hare's Ear with a smaller, brighter, wire-style fly, such as a size 14 red or chartreuse Copper John on the point sixteen inches below it. If I could get away without adding weight on the leader, that's the way I fished it, but I didn't hesitate to add split shot or even twist-ons (ribbonlike strips of lead) above the first or between the two flies or both if I felt it was necessary to get them down on the bottom. I was aware that some of my pals were piecing together

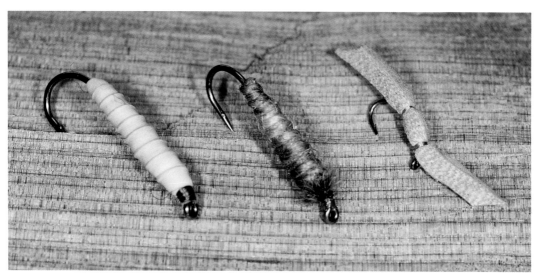

The Rubber Band Fly (left) and Burlap Fly (middle) were standard imitations for crane-fly larvae on the South Platte River in the 1970s and 1980s. More recently, the Chamois Leech (right) has become a popular crane-fly larva imitation because it's active in the water and more closely represents a crane-fly larva in a non-defensive swimming mode.

rigs that included various-sized lengths of lead-core line to get the flies down, but I found it unnecessary for fishing close to the banks where I concentrated much of my early efforts.

If I found concentrations of earthworms, aquatic worms, or crane-fly larvae in my samples, I'd switch to a two-fly rig with a large, weighted, worm imitation and a second smaller weighted worm of a distinctly different color. Sometimes I might switch out one of the worms for a crane-fly larva imitation or fish two crane-fly larva imitations of different sizes and colors.

Many years ago, the Rubber Band Fly was a favorite crane-fly imitation on Colorado's South Platte River near where I live. The locals called the crane-fly larvae that got flushed out of the banks and streambed during the high-volume springtime water

releases rockworms, and the imitation was an easy fly to tie. Initially it consisted of a rubber band wrapped around the hook shank with black thread. Later renditions included some lead wire under the rubber band for added weight and a bit of brown hackle. The fly was the first example I saw of what would eventually become a whole class of latex-bodied imitations. The fly was successful because the rubber band matched the color and segmentation of a natural crane fly in the withdrawn or defensive position it often assumes when caught in the drift. At the time, the soft rubber body was a new sensation to the trout too.

Later another successful crane-fly larvae pattern called a Burlap Fly showed up on the river. Like the Rubber Band Fly, the Burlap Fly was simple. It was nothing more than a strand of burlap from a burlap bag wrapped around the hook shank that had been weighted with lead wire. Some tiers used felt pens to color the burlap to more closely resemble the natural, but even the straight burlap was a good imitation of the natural's color and segmentation. It has been years since I've fished either one of these imitations, but I suspect they might still be effective. My current crane-fly larvae imitation of choice is the Chamois Leech. It's similar to the other crane-fly larvae patterns because of its simplicity. The fly is nothing more that a thin strip of pliable, tanned leather tied to a hook. I use either an off-white or golden brown color, although it seems like every Chamois Leech devotee has a favorite color.

The one question I've never resolved was whether the trout take any of these imitations for an actual crane-fly larva at all since I did not come up with that many crane flies when I sampled stomach contents. My instinct is that the trout are familiar with crane-fly larvae and will take them whenever the opportunity presents itself, but high water conditions don't necessarily guarantee that they will be in the drift. It might also be that a crane-fly larva imitation is just a good general representation of any number of trout foods that might get washed into the river during high flows. It's also interesting to note that two of the larger aquatic crane-fly larvae commonly found in trout streams (genera *Hexatoma* and *Tipula*) appear considerably thinner and longer when they come out of their more compact defensive positions. Both of these crane-fly larvae appear to swim with a kind of undulating motion when unthreatened. The Chamois Leech is longer and thinner and more active in the water than most crane-fly larvae imitations, which may account for its high-water effectiveness. A brown or tan marabou leech is another option if you're after the undulating movement of a crane-fly larva on the move.

NYMPHING TACTICS FOR HIGH WATER

Nymphing tactics for high water are similar to those used under more normal conditions. The key is to get the flies down, which can be accomplished by either using larger, heavily weighted flies or attaching some form of weight to the leader. The best place to begin your high-water nymphing is along the bank on your side of the river. This is practical because the river is often unwadable when the water is high, and you'll be forced to fish from the bank anyway. In addition, the two- or three-foot zone close to the bank often has the softer water that the trout seek out during runoff or flood conditions.

This is the perfect situation to apply your short-line nymphing skills. It's as easy as casting a single or two-fly rig far enough upstream for it to sink to the bottom and then allowing it to bounce along the streambed as it drifts down in front of you and then a bit farther downstream. I never have more than ten feet of fly line out past my tip-top line guide when I short-line high water and typically have just two or three feet. My main goal on every drift is to stay in contact with the flies by keeping any slack line out of the system. I accomplish this by lifting the rod tip as the flies drift downstream toward me and then lowering the tip when they pass by me and continue the drift downstream. You should have just the barest amount of tension in the leader to help you sense more subtle strikes, which

Nymphing large, weighted nymph patterns close in to the bank is a good strategy when the water is high and off-color.

surprisingly are not uncommon when fishing nymphs in slower-moving high water. (See chapter 1 for more information on detecting strikes by feel.)

If you feel like you're missing strikes or just not in touch with your nymph imitations, you might want to take a page out of the Czech nymphing guidebook and hold your rod tip closer to the water and gently guide the flies downstream on a tight line. The tight line will help define subtle strikes that might otherwise be hard to detect. Unlike most of my pals, I don't use a strike indicator for high-water, short-line nymphing situations because I think it detracts from my sense of feel. But I have no doubt that a good indicator nympher will fish this kind of water as well as anyone.

In most cases, you'll be able to get right up on the trout without being detected because the off-color water will prevent the trout from seeing you. How close you do get, of course, depends on degrees, and if you think the water is clear enough for you to be detected by the trout, it will pay to revert to stealth mode. When you are working the banks, pay special attention to any clumps of grass, rock, or logs that protrude into the current that can act as a velocity barrier. Remember that you can use the tip of your rod to guide the drift around these velocity barriers to help the flies search out trout. If you find that the flies are drifting into undercut banks, hold the rod out over the water to guide them through the drift. Holding the rod over the water will also

The lower water volume in side channels or braided areas is often sought out by trout trying to avoid heavy flows in the main channel.

The slower-moving water of a side channel is an ideal place to employ short-line nymphing tactics when the water is high and discolored.

The calmer water behind a submerged rock may hold a trout when flows are high.

Trout often stack up in the slower water on the downstream side of an island or gravel bar when flows are high.

FINDING HIGH-WATER TROUT

When rivers are swollen with spring runoff, trout seek out these areas of slower-moving water.

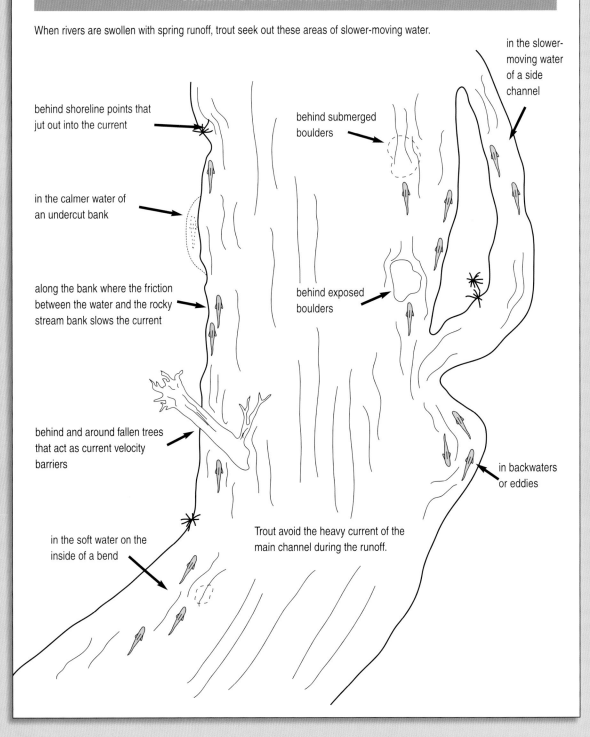

in the slower-moving water of a side channel

behind shoreline points that jut out into the current

behind submerged boulders

in the calmer water of an undercut bank

along the bank where the friction between the water and the rocky stream bank slows the current

behind exposed boulders

behind and around fallen trees that act as current velocity barriers

in backwaters or eddies

in the soft water on the inside of a bend

Trout avoid the heavy current of the main channel during the runoff.

help you lever any trout you manage to hook into the main current where you will have a better shot at playing them.

In addition to working the bank on your side of the river, you should target any side channel, backwater, or the inside of bends where the current slows. I will often pinch on an indicator when I fish a side channel or backwater because I want to cover all of it, and I think the buoyant indicator greatly increases my chances of getting a good dead-drift when I'm nymphing a longer line.

Although the banks, side channels, and back eddies are my main targets, I always take the opportunity to make a few drifts behind any visible or submerged larger rocks I can detect within casting range and along any submerged gravel or sandbars. Trout will sometimes stack up in the stillwater at the downstream end of a bar or island just above where the two currents come together.

The only change I make for high-water nymphing is to scale up my tackle a bit. A 9-foot graphite is about right, but rather than the 4-weight or 5-weight that I might choose for normal water conditions I'll often bump up to a 6- to 8-weight rod depending on conditions. The heavier rod may not necessarily be required for the actual nymphing but more for fighting fish in the heavier water. I beef up the leader too, which I like to be 9 or 10 feet long with a 2X to 4X fluorocarbon tippet, depending on conditions.

HIGH-STICKING STREAMERS

A major turning point in my short-line success occurred when a friend introduced me to high-stick streamer fishing during the spring runoff. The actual technique used to fish the streamer was almost identical to the way I fished nymphs close in to the bank, except that I often made a point to add a few twitches of action to the fly as it drifted downstream. It was also important to follow the fly's drift downstream with the rod tip and then lift or let the current lift the fly to the surface at the end of the dead drift.

Although the high-stick techniques used for high-water nymphing and streamer fishing are quite similar, streamers have some characteristics that make them a very powerful fly choice when the water is high and discolored. The first is obvious—streamers are larger flies and trout are predominantly sight hunters. When the water is dirty, it only makes sense that a larger fly will be more visible. It also makes sense that a trout might choose to nail a larger food source

High-sticking a large, weighted streamer close in to the bank is the most versatile and productive method for catching trout when the water is high and off-color.

Adding a flashy material such as blue Krystal Flash to this black Woolly Bugger increases its effectiveness when the water is high and dirty.

Adding a Muddler head to a Zonker-style fly creates what some fly tiers call a Zuddler. The Zuddler's larger head creates a bigger profile, which is easier for trout to see when the water is dirty.

especially if it is easier to catch. Of course, you are probably thinking, why would a streamer that most commonly imitates some sort of baitfish be *easier* to catch than, say, a large nymph that's been kicked into the drift by high water?

The reasoning is that although the streamer is imitating a baitfish, you're not actively *swinging* it on a tight line. A streamer that's actively fished on a tight line may imitate a fleeing baitfish or simply supply the motion to trigger a strike reaction from the trout. A weighted streamer that is dead-drifted in front of a trout most likely imitates a crippled, wounded, or dead baitfish. And it makes sense that there might be more beat-up baitfish when the water is high. It only figures that baitfish that get inadvertently pushed out into heavy flow may be injured or killed when they are thrust against objects by the strong current. It's even more likely that they simply become disoriented and vulnerable when pushed around by the high water volume. A smaller fish in this condition is easy pickings for a trout.

When I first started high-sticking streamers in high-water conditions, I pretty much stuck with the streamer patterns that I used under more typical flow conditions, although I did go a few hook sizes larger especially if the water was dirty. My two favorite flies were rather heavily weighted black size 8 to 4 Woolly Buggers and size 4 or 6 Zonkers tied with a silver Mylar body and black rabbit strip wing. I liked both these patterns because they were easy to tie and used materials that were active in the water on a dead drift.

As time went by and I began talking to other high-water fly fishers I'd run into on the river, I modified the patterns a bit and added a few new ones. The most effective modification that I made was adding blue Flashabou to the tail of the black Woolly Bugger and then also as a lateral line under the palmer hackle of the pattern. I made this modification at the urging of several pals who insisted that the blue and the flash would increase the productivity of the pattern, and I believe to this day that it does.

Although I fooled around quite a bit with the Zonker, the only modification I found that seemed to have some effect was to add a Muddler Minnow–style deer-hair head to create what is now known as a Zuddler. I added that after I'd read a magazine article that said that a Muddler Minnow was a good bet for high, dirty water conditions because the deer-hair head pushed more water and made it easier for the trout to detect with its lateral line. I'm still not sure I buy the lateral line logic because I think trout are first and

foremost sight hunters, but I do think the Muddler head beefs up the fly's silhouette, making it easier to see in dirty water, which makes it easier for trout to find.

Tackle for High-Sticking Streamers

I never high-stick streamers with anything less than a stout 9-foot, 6-weight rod with a 9- or 10-foot 0X to 3X leader. I typically use a nylon leader, but if I think abrasion will be an issue, I switch to fluorocarbon. One subtlety to watch for when you're dead-drifting a streamer occurs in soft-water zones close to the bank. Sometimes a trout will nail the weighted streamer as it falls to the bottom in the slower-moving water. This isn't the kind of take you anticipate in high water, and it can be easy to miss. If you don't have too much slack in the system, you may actually feel the often subtle strike. You can sometimes detect the strike almost by instinct when the fly line or leader is on the water's surface and just doesn't act right. More than anything, if you maintain an awareness that you *could* get a strike when the fly is dropping and try to stay in contact with it, you'll probably pick up on the strikes. You might also try executing a short lift if you think you have a strike. The lift will take any slack out of the system, and you'll feel the fish on the other end, at which point you need to remember to set the hook.

Also be advised that some of the takes you'll get once the fly begins its drift could be quite subtle. Remember, the trout figures that your imitation is a gift—a meal he doesn't have to chase down. You'll need to manage the slack and stay in contact with the fly to be successful. When you do get the occasional slam-dunk strike, figure that it's a gift to you—most of your hookups won't come that way.

I sometimes add a trailing fly 8 to 18 inches behind the streamer when I high-stick. It's a rig that will tangle up now and then, but I think it's worth the tangles because you can put two different fly types in front of the fish. I'll often put a Zuddler first and trail a smaller black Woolly Bugger behind it. Sometimes I mix it up with a Woolly or Zuddler trailed by a flashy wire-bodied nymph imitation or an old reliable like a Beadhead Flashback Gold-Ribbed Hare's Ear.

I like high-sticking streamers in high-water conditions because it helps me stay in touch with the flies, and that helps me detect strikes. But there are high-water situations where you will be able to open up a bit and fish more traditional streamer tactics. When these tight-line tactics are feasible, your greatest challenge will be getting the fly down. For most fly fishers, this will mean some sort of high density sink-tip fly line or even a full sink line for special conditions or big water.

Since I don't usually fish big water during the runoff, I've adopted an abbreviated sink-tip rig to use on the small- to average-size rivers that I fish during the spring runoff. I started off with high-density sink-tip fly line and then cut the head back to 4 feet and added a short, 3- or 4-foot basic leader. Other fly fishers, especially on the West Coast, made the ultimate high-density sinking heads with a 2- to 4-foot section of lead-core line attached by a loop-to-loop connection to the fly line. This setup will effectively drag streamers along the streambed even in moderate to heavy current. The downside is that

it's miserable to cast. More recent refinements in high-density mini-sinking heads are a reasonable middle ground. They come closer to lead-core densities and are a bit easier to cast. I haven't switched to either the lead-core or the mini-sinking heads mainly because my older, cut-off, high-density sink-tip line works fine for the conditions where I use it. If I did find myself on bigger water or in a situation where I needed to modify this rig, I think I would do my best to get by with the mini-sinking head if at all possible.

I initially used a 4-foot-long section of 8-pound-test Maxima Chameleon for a leader on my shortened sink-tip rig. Later I tried the same length leader in 8-pound-test fluorocarbon. In terms of performance, I haven't really noticed a difference between the two materials, so I more or less use them interchangeably. What I have noticed is that if I'm going to fish a sink tip, it pays to keep the leader short and use a weighted streamer pattern. The combination of the short sink tip and weighted fly gets the rig down fast and keeps it down. This setup is deadly when cast up against an undercut bank and stripped and wiggled a few times as it swings in the current. It also hits pay dirt when you quarter it down and across stream and allow it to slowly swing through the inside of a bend. Although I prefer to high-stick the softer water close to the bank, the sink-tip streamer rig can be productive when cast straight upstream along the bank and then stripped as fast as possible downstream.

TACTICS FOR HIGH, MUDDY WATER

An interesting piece of the high-water puzzle came to light when I found myself trying to understand some just plain muddy water.

In this case, it was toward the end of Colorado's spring runoff, and the river was so dirty that I could barely see my wading shoes in 10 inches of water. These are the kinds of conditions that create terror in a fly fisher. You want to run back to your truck screaming or at least just go home and tie flies. If you decide to fish at all, let's just say your expectations aren't going to be too high. In fact, the most difficult part of the endeavor may be trying to muster up a semblance of concentration. Nonetheless, I decided to rig up anyway and actually ran into another fly fisher when I walked down to the river. He half-smiled and grimaced at me and said, "I guess I'm not the only nutcase trying to fly-fish muddy water, but it's still better than work."

When we parted and headed our separate ways to the river, I wondered how he would do and even if it mattered to him. In a lot of ways, horrible fishing conditions actually take the pressure off. I was reminded that over the years, most of the fly fishers I'd run into when the river was muddy were just going through the motions, although once in a while there was one or two who were really trying to figure out what they needed to do to catch a trout. I've always made a point to pick those anglers' brains. I found that we usually agreed that whatever fly you used it should be heavily weighted, big, and black. Our reliance on the color black as a base for our flies probably came out of the old fly-fishing adage: dark water, dark fly; light water, light fly. And it did make sense that a dark-colored fly would stand out best in dirty water.

Most of the more serious muddy-water fly fishers also agreed that using flies with a large Muddler-style head couldn't hurt, if only to create a more visible profile. One of them was experimenting with various kinds of rattles in his flies, but it hadn't resulted in any huge increase in strikes. We all seemed to favor flies with some kind of active material such as rabbit hair or marabou to create the illusion of life or at least attract the trout's attention. Finally, we agreed to a person, that dead-drifting streamers and nymphs close in to the bank almost always worked better than swinging streamers.

Large streamers that are black with a secondary lighter color are more likely to be visible to trout in muddy water conditions.

I still basically adhere to those principles, but in addition I keep an eye open for any water that for some reason appears to be less roily. Sometimes the dynamics of the current flow will partially clear the water in a small section of river, and that attracts trout. I believe it's because the trout are primarily sight feeders, and they will try to find water where the visibility is better. In really muddy conditions, that better visibility may only be the difference between eight inches and a foot and a half, but that can be important to a sight feeder. When I find this kind of clearer water, I make a point to fish it more thoroughly and will take the time to change flies and experiment with different tactics. But that's about as far as my strategy goes other than believing that the most difficult task of the day may simply be finding trout. And to do that you will probably have to cover water, concentrate, and maintain a positive attitude.

FLIES THAT TROUT CAN SEE IN MUDDY WATER

Fly fishing for trout in muddy water isn't exactly a hotbed of new ideas and techniques. The most compelling recent work has actually been done by a steelhead fisherman in the Northwest who fishes gear rather than flies. Colin Kageyama is an optometrist who used optical filters to simulate water tint and murkiness and then checked his results with an underwater camera in the actual conditions. He found that his filter system could accurately predict the degree of visibility that various colors have at different depths and water conditions. The obvious advantage of the filter system is that Kageyama could look at the color of a steel-

head lure in the comfort of his home and predict how visible it would be to a steelhead in a variety of water conditions. And that's important because steelhead, like trout, are predominantly sight feeders.

Kageyama verified the results of his filter studies by putting different-colored steelhead lures on a board and then photographing them at different depths. The underwater photographs confirmed that many of the colors turned black due to color shifts caused when the water absorbed light. Those were difficult to see, but a few remained bright. The effect was further influenced by the background behind the lures (light or dark) and the tint of the water (blue, green, or muddy).

Kageyama ultimately expanded his studies to include fly-tying materials and shared the results in his book, *What Trout See: Understanding Optics and Color Shifts for Designing Lures and Flies* (Frank Amato Publications, 1999). Fly fishers weren't too surprised that Kageyama found that black shows up well at short ranges in muddy water because of its high contrast with the background (the muddy water). But a real surprise was that black became difficult to see in dirty water at greater distances, on dark days, and when the water is moderately cloudy. The real kicker was that you have to always consider the background against which the trout see the fly. If the trout is looking up toward the surface in muddy water, your black Woolly Bugger is going to stand out, but if he's looking down toward the stream bottom, which tends to create a dark background, the fly is going to be more difficult to see.

Those observations seemed to indicate that you would have to use a different fly

Large, weighted conehead Zonkers that utilize contrasting colors known to be most visible to trout in muddy water conditions increase the odds of a strike. The use of truly fluorescent materials may further enhance the fly's effectiveness.

A black Zuddler using chartreuse as a secondary color for the body and a flashy gold conehead creates a large profile fly that is highly visible to trout when the water is off-color or muddy.

Ben Furmisky's Gunni Special incorporates all the ingredients necessary for a fly to be highly visible to trout in dirty water—it's black with fluorescent chartreuse as a secondary color, incorporates active chartreuse rubber legs, and has a shiny gold bead.

pattern based on *where* the trout is looking, which is obviously impossible to know. Kageyama's answer was that you design a fly that has a secondary, contrasting color. By using two contrasting colors, the fly will be visible against dark or light backgrounds because where one color is difficult to see the other color will be visible and vice versa. That means you have a chance that the trout will see your fly at longer and shorter distances and under light and dark conditions. For muddy waters, the best overall color combination appears to be black and fluorescent chartreuse with a bit of flashy gold. Other secondary color choices to go with black are white or yellow.

An important observation that Kageyama made was that true fluorescent colors can be quite visible under a variety of situations, but he cautions that many fly-tying materials that appear to be very bright or fluorescent in room lighting aren't as bright as fluorescent paints or beads when actually tested underwater. (A true fluorescent color absorbs high-energy, short-wavelength light such as ultraviolet and reemits it as a lower energy longer wavelength visible color that has a high reflectance value. Conventional color is created by reflected light only.) Kageyama suggests that dye lots, bleaching process, the time/temperature of the dying process, and the fact that different parts of natural materials take up dyes differently cause quality-control issues, which in turn may cause changes in the underwater visibility of a supposedly fluorescent material.

As it turns out, the most reliable way to capitalize on Kageyama's research when designing fluorescent flies for muddy water is to use fluorescent painted eyes, beads, or coneheads because it's more likely that these painted fluorescent colors will be truly fluorescent and able to maintain their fluorescent characteristics underwater.

If you believe that trout are predominantly sight hunters and the ultimate challenge when fishing dirty water is to design flies that the trout can see, Kageyama's work is bound to excite you. It isn't difficult to modify your basic dirty-water fly selection to reflect his findings. Consider adding gold or fluorescent chartreuse, yellow, or even red coneheads to your black Woolly Buggers and maybe even some gold Flashabou in the tail. Zonkers or Zuddlers can also be brightened up with the fluorescent coneheads, a gold Mylar braid body, and black rabbit strip added for contrast. You might also want to experiment with fluorescent chartreuse and yellow rabbit strips against a silver or gold braid body. The main thing to keep in mind is the idea of a secondary contrasting color.

Surprisingly, when I looked at my latest Kageyama-inspired muddy-water fly modifications, it occurred to me that the idea of contrasting colors in streamers is not all new. Thoughtful fly tiers who imitate baitfish know that the top of the real baitfish is often dark and the bottom is typically lighter. It might be that in addition to having a fly that looks like the natural, those contrasting colors may also make the imitations more visible against different background colors, but that is hit-or-miss depending on the color and depth of the water. But what is new is a system for determining which colors are most visible under certain conditions. And that can build confidence when you're trying to come up with new patterns. I learned a long time ago that if I can modify or design a fly pattern that gives me confidence, I'll fish that pattern longer and concentrate more when I do fish it. And sometimes that's as important as all the science and the magic.

I recently surveyed the streamer selections of a number of the major fly manufacturers at a fly-fishing trade show. About half of the patterns relied on a single basic color and some kind of highly reflective flashy material. Some patterns employed a contrasting color, but the proportion of the secondary color was small and may not have been as effective as it would be if it was represented in a closer to 50/50 proportion. When I asked some of the fly designers what the best patterns for muddy water were most of them drew a blank, with the exception of Gunnison River guide Ben Furimsky, who went straight to the bin and picked up his Gunni Special. "This one works the best when the water's dirty," he said. I held the fly in my hand. The Woolly Bugger–inspired design was definitely weighted, but even more important, it was black and chartreuse with chartreuse rubber legs. The finishing touch was a gold bead. It couldn't have been much closer to Kageyama's predictions for high visibility in muddy water.

SPECIAL HIGH-WATER SITUATIONS AND TACTICS

Tailwaters
Every tailwater fly fisher has a story about when the water came up. Of course, there are the often humorous tales of the fishermen who failed to notice the rising water and had to hightail it to high ground. But aside from the comedy, another thread often runs through these stories—the trout

really seem to turn on right when the flow comes up.

I first noticed this many years ago when I fished the Traun River in Austria. A small hydroelectric dam made periodic releases that never raised the water more than a foot or so. The first time I saw the water coming up I figured that was it for the day, but just as I

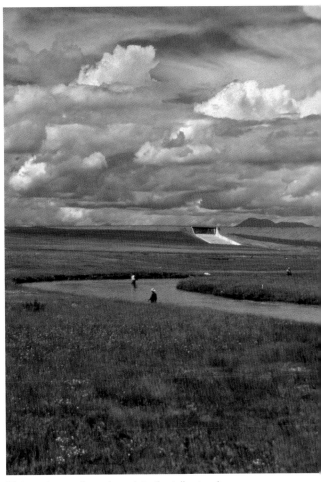

Water releases from dams into the tailwater rivers below them create artificial high-water conditions. Trout sometimes feed voraciously right when the water comes up.

Many tailwaters have large populations of aquatic worms that are unavailable to the trout. When water is released, the high flows often kick the worms into the drift where the trout feed heavily on them.

turned to wade to the shore I saw a rise and then another and another. It wasn't long before there were a dozen steady risers within casting range.

I didn't see any insects on the surface, and it was hard to believe that the water release would trigger a hatch, but the riseforms told me that the trout were taking something just below the surface. I tied on a general-purpose soft hackle and started casting at rises. It wasn't long before I was tight on a native brown trout. I came to find during my brief visit to the river the same thing happened every day at the same time. I vowed to never leave a tailwater again just because the water came up!

A similar effect often occurs on the South Platte River near my home in Colorado. When I first witnessed a water release in person, I once again figured the fishing was over if only because the water was filled with debris, but that changed quickly when my fishing pal shouted, "Break out the worms!" I found out that he meant San Juan Worms and that you could catch a trout on just about every drift that didn't get fouled up with debris. Upon reflection, it seemed obvious that the high water dislodged some of the river's abundant supply of usually unavailable aquatic worms and the trout went to town on them.

Since that first experience, I've fished the releases many times with similar results. Of course, the other side of the coin on a release is that the feeding frenzy often goes off within a half hour and things seem to shut down completely until the trout get reoriented to the new flows. Most of the time they get pushed into the banks where standard high-water tactics can be applied.

I've heard other stories of boaters riding the release wave of a hydroelectric dam's water release and fly-fishing it with great success for miles downstream. The point here is that you shouldn't necessarily throw in the towel just because the water comes up at your favorite tailwater. When you see the stream rising, make sure you are safe and then start thinking about your high-water tactics—imitate a larger trout food source that might now be available to the trout, stay in touch with the fly by high-sticking, and move to the softer water along the banks once the new water level has been established. If you find yourself on a tailwater where really extreme releases occur, be sure to check out any tributaries where the trout might head to get out of the heavy flows.

Dry Flies

The last thing most of us think about when the water is high and off-color is fishing dry flies, and that's probably good because you're going to be more consistently effective using the subsurface techniques we've talked about. But that doesn't mean you can't occasionally catch trout on dries. If you fish off-color water enough, you may see a few hatches of insects, but you probably won't see any rises. The best strategy at these times is to imitate the emerging form of the insect and fish it below the surface.

A better time to break out a dry fly is when you encounter high, off-color, but not muddy, water. If you happen to observe hatching insects and actually see a trout or two rise in a backwater, you might be able to match the hatch, but that's pretty uncommon. The more likely scenario is that you won't see any rises, but you'll be able to raise a few trout on attractor patterns. I like large dry-fly patterns that produce a broad silhouette on the water from the trout's point of view. Flies like the Convertible, Turck's Tarantula, or even a bushy Stimulator all produce this kind of broad silhouette and are visible even when the water is off-color. I target my casts to every likely looking spot

TROUT'S VIEW OF A HIGH-WATER DRY FLY

Turck's Tarantula is a highly visible dry fly that can be productive when fished along the banks when the water is high and off-color.

One reason that the Turck's Tarantula and other similar fly patterns are successful in high, off-color water conditions is that they sit down on the water's surface, which creates a broad profile that is highly visible from the trout's point of view.

in the soft-water zone within two feet of the bank. I also look for any clumps of grass protruding into the flow that might make a good holding spot for a trout or the dead spots behind boulders, eddies, backwaters, and the inside of bends. I usually make a cast or two, and if I don't get a response, I move upstream. Although I tend to look at fishing dry flies as more of a diversion when the water is high and off-color, I've been surprised at their effectiveness on several occasions. And that goes to prove, once again, that versatility and the willingness to try something new never hurts when things get tough on the river.

So that's what I know about high water, and I'll understand if you choose to avoid such conditions. I don't really seek them out either. But high water is a lot like the weather. If I decide I'm going fishing, I don't let the weather or high water stop me. No one is saying that it will be easy. But at least you're on the river.

CHAPTER 7

Small-Stream Finesse

Finding and fishing backcountry streams and beaver ponds

It's the latter part of June, and I can't wait for summertime to arrive in Colorado's Rocky Mountains. In the past, I've always declared the Fourth of July as the unofficial start of my high-country fishing season, but that changed four or five years ago when a drought opened up the high country much sooner than any of us had ever seen. Of course, it was a mixed blessing for fly fishermen. We had early access to the backcountry but not much water. I still remember the worst year of the drought because it was the only time in all the years I've lived in Colorado that there was no snow on the mountains in late spring. I was up in the high country then and did a 360-degree slow spin, and *all* the peaks were dry. I won't try to explain how frightening that was to a high-country angler.

I won't digress into the climate change predictions that we've all been hearing about

and the politics that go with them. All I can say is that the drought loosened its grip on us in Colorado, and we've been doing okay. Unfortunately the same isn't true for some other Rocky Mountain states that have been experiencing drought conditions for close to a decade now.

So, anyway, here I am up in the mountains a few weeks earlier than I should be trying to sneak in as much backcountry fishing as I can get. . . .

The small stream I'm fishing today flows under of a canopy of Engelmann spruce and subalpine fir on national forest land. The access is not difficult, but you do have to travel in four-wheel drive for a little way before you park the truck and head out on foot. The real key is that you actually head out on foot. I know for a fact that if you just walk a half mile up almost any small stream that crosses a forest road in Colorado you proba-

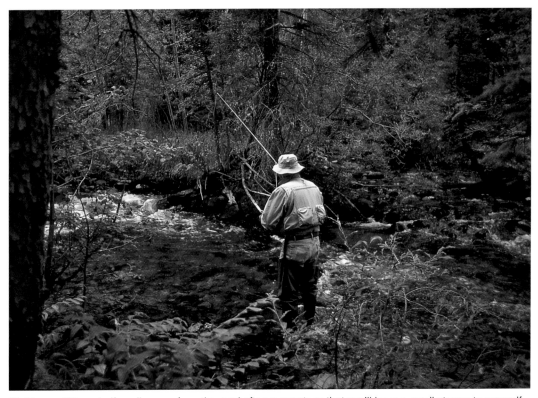

Walking as little as half a mile away from the road often guarantees that you'll have a small stream to yourself.

bly won't see another human being for the rest of the day.

I'm alone today mostly because it has become my habit, and on a more practical level, it's just not that easy to find someone to fish with during the week. Other than that, I can't exactly explain why I've become a small-stream loner. For a while I thought I'd just become greedy. When I fish alone I don't have to worry about the choreography of leapfrogging upstream past a pal so we both get a shot at unfished water. I was always susceptible to the little infidelities that go with that—like seeing an especially sexy plunge pool in the other guy's supposedly unfished leapfrog zone, surreptitiously high-grading it,

and then not 'fessing up later in the day when he comments that there weren't any fish in one really good-looking pool.

The exception I will make to my habit of solitary fishing is my friend John Gierach. We've fished the backcountry together for more than thirty years and manage an almost effortless angling harmony when we are together. The plan is always the same. We simply say that we'll meet at the truck if we don't see each other on the stream, although invariably we do cross paths several times during the course of the day. But that doesn't necessarily mean that we stop fishing or say anything. When we do, it usually amounts to sitting down on the bank and watching the water or maybe eating our lunches or mentioning an especially nice brookie one of us has managed to catch.

As it turns out, my timing today, on this stream, isn't too bad. The water is still a little high, but it's clear. Odds are it's also a bit cold because there are still a few snowdrifts here and there. That might put the bite off a bit, but these trout are opportunists. If they can find a sunny spot where the water is a bit warmer or if something remotely resembling food drifts by them, they'll probably take it. Winter is always around the corner in the mountains, and the trout know it.

I'll start off with my standard small-stream rig. It hasn't changed much for many years. I like an easy-to-see attractor dry-fly pattern like a size 14 Standard Royal Coachman or Royal Coachman Trude. A lot of other flies will serve equally well—a Rio Grande King

Trude, House and Lot, Wulff, Parachute Hare's Ear, or Elk Hair Caddis. If it were a little later in the season, I might go with a favorite of mine, the Yellow Stimulator, because it mimics a hopper or any other of a smattering of light-colored insects I sometimes see on the water here.

Whenever possible, I try to fish a single dry fly on small streams just because I like the simplicity of it. My more practical fly fisherman logic behind the single fly is that I don't get hung up as much as I do when I fish a dropper off the dry. I don't doubt that a dropper will account for more fish under almost any conditions, but that doesn't always override the sense of economy that I get from fishing the single dry fly. But having said that, I will start with the dry fly and dropper today because it's early in the season, and I have convinced myself that the

The best small-stream trout aren't necessarily found in the prime lies.

trout may not be looking up yet. And besides, I've had the jones all winter to hold and then release a backcountry trout.

Once I'm all rigged up and set to go, I pick a spot that looks prime. There is a riffle that narrows and drops into a small pool. My plan is to start at the shallow, bottom end of the pool and fish my way up until I hit the sweet spot in the deeper water under the current line. It took me a long time to learn to start at the bottom of a pool like this because I knew there would almost always be a fish in the sweet spot and couldn't wait to try to catch it. I changed my ways when my friend Mike Price showed me that the very best fish in a small stream sometimes aren't in the prime spot where you think they should be.

Mike literally picks a small stream apart. He puts a fly on every square inch of water that has even a remote possibility of holding a trout. If it looks particularly good, he may put two or three casts over it, but the point is that he catches fish in water that may be only five or six inches deep, under brush, behind submerged stones that barely disrupt the current line, and from the indistinct foam lines that are everywhere in a small stream. And it doesn't take him much time to cover all those spots. His efficient casts remind me of the way a snake uses its tongue to constantly test and sample everything around it.

So I make my first cast to an offbeat little riffle at the bottom of the pool. The only characteristic that sets it apart is that it's lit up by a rectangular patch of sunlight. The water's probably no more than eight inches deep, but nonetheless a seven-inch brookie nails the dry fly on the first drift. I wonder if maybe the trout are looking up or if this is just a quirk. The great thing is that I'll have the rest of the day to find out.

During that time, I'll probably think about some of the things I've learned about fishing small mountain streams when the usual fly combinations don't work, or maybe I'll remember some of the larger backcountry trout I've landed and what made them different, or even how I've learned to use topographical maps and aerial or satellite photos to find productive small streams. I'll go through all of those things and dream about the season ahead of me.

SMALL-STREAM BASICS

Before we can talk seriously about small-stream finesse it might not hurt to review the basics of fly-fishing small streams and some ways for you to tune-up your small-stream game.

I've often heard fly fishers say that small streams are simply microcosms of larger trout rivers, and that's true as far as it goes. Small-stream trout can generally be found in water types similar to water types where you'd expect to find them in bigger rivers. I look for upland small-stream trout in miniature riffles, glides, and plunge pools. But that's where I draw the line on the similarities because over the years I've learned that small-stream trout sometimes hang out in *different* parts of these water types.

The most important difference between a small stream and a river is the availability of hiding cover. Big water has plenty of places where trout can hide from predators. Most runs and many riffles are deep enough for the trout's natural coloring to camouflage it. Even large trout can disappear in the deeper holes.

Hiding cover for trout is more readily available in a big river than it is in a small stream.

A small stream is different. Deep water is at a premium. When it isn't available trout may take cover in shady areas, under overhanging branches, around submerged brush, or below undercut banks. Larger-than-average small-stream trout almost always dominate feeding lies that are close to some kind of hiding cover. When hiding cover is not available, trout risk detection in feeding lies that might be as shallow as a few inches or even out in the open under bright skies. In terms of spookiness, these small-stream trout put their big-river brothers to shame.

The probability that small-stream trout will be skittish means that your approach to the water may be the most important thing you do all day. I used to never worry too much about my approach because I always caught trout. One of the great joys of upland stream fishing is that a simple attractor dry-fly pattern will often catch trout all day. Of course, those trout tend to be universally small with only the occasional monster ten-incher.

I was happy with just catching smaller fish until I got to thinking about what I call the streakers. Most small-stream fishers are familiar with the occasional trout that streaks away far upstream from them. I always wrote those fish off as having overly sensitive lateral lines. Streakers are especially common around the marshy areas near beaver ponds where the spongy banks telegraph anything but the most carefully placed steps. But

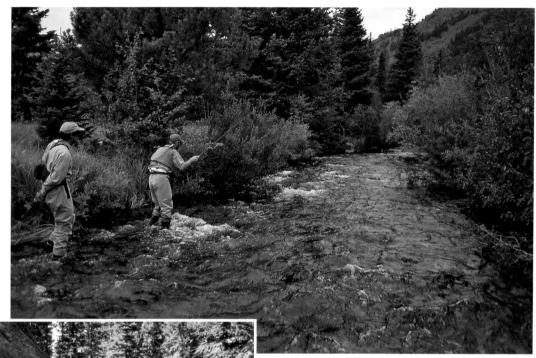

Deep water hiding cover is at a premium in a small stream. When it isn't available, trout may take cover in shady areas under overhanging brush.

A deep pool that is also near a feeding lie is prime habitat for small-stream trout. This pool has the added advantage of being in the shade most of the day.

clumsy wading or a shoddy approach anywhere on a small stream will also send them on their way.

One day I was fishing one of my favorite stretches of small water in the nearby national forest when a fish streaked out twenty yards upstream from me. For fun I decided that I'd try to make an approach and presentation that didn't send any trout streaking for cover. I very carefully lowered my profile and used the streamside vegetation to break

Small-stream trout are often skittish. Wherever possible, try to use the streamside vegetation to break up your silhouette when making the approach to your casting position.

up my silhouette. Wherever possible I stayed in the shadows and didn't wade unless absolutely necessary.

As I got closer to a stretch of totally undisturbed water, I hunkered down and finished the approach on all fours. When I spotted a nice slick of slower-moving water up against a grassy bank, I worked myself into a casting position. I then carefully cast my trusty size 14 Yellow Stimulator up onto the grass and pulled it off into the water. A 12-inch cutthroat trout exploded on it. I was amazed. This was water that I knew well and where I had never caught anything larger than 8 or 9 inches. It occurred to me that maybe the streakers were trying to tell me that I was spooking all the good fish! I now take the

utmost care when approaching prime small-stream water, and I can testify that I've been introduced to some trout that I would never have expected to be residing in a brook.

Another aspect of small-stream angling you might want to brush up on is your water reading skills. If you can't visually confirm whether or not a trout occupies a stretch of water, take a page from Mike Price's book and cast a fly to it. It doesn't matter if it's a tiny slick the size of a coffee cup saucer or a ribbon of riffle just two inches deep. Float a fly over it.

You should give more obvious spots like small plunge pools additional attention. I'm especially attentive to the thin collar of whitewater that often rims the downstream

Make a point to fish any water that has even a remote chance of holding a trout. Some of the best fish come from places where you'd least expect to find them.

Many small-stream fly fishers pass by spots like this shaded pool where the overhanging brush makes a presentation difficult. That's a mistake because these are the kind of lies that often hold the better trout simply because they don't get fished very often.

or tail section of a plunge pool. Once you've worked that, put a few flies out on the slick, and for the finale, work the head where the water plunges into the pool. Deeper runs, slots, and glides should all get peppered with casts, as should hard-to-reach slicks tucked up under overhanging brush.

The most important element of your small-stream philosophy should always be if you can't see into the water and ascertain for certain that a trout isn't holding there, assume that one is and make a cast or two. You can be confident that if a trout is nearby and you make a decent cast, it will strike. Always

The soft water up along a rock has all the ingredients necessary to hold small-stream trout—deeper, slow-moving water, shade, and a current tongue close by to deliver food.

The foam-speckled water directly below the large rock is the kind of out-of-the-way place that can hold a surprisingly nice trout because most small-stream anglers pass it by.

make your searching casts *before* you get close enough to spook a trout that might be there.

It may sound obvious, but the beauty of fishing a small stream is the very fact that it is small. You have the luxury of covering any water that has even the remote chance of holding a trout. Over time you will learn where trout most often hang out, but always fish all the possibilities. You'll be surprised

The patience to deliver a fly under difficult circumstances may be rewarded with a larger-than-average trout.

how many trout show themselves in lies that you might have passed over as unproductive.

TACKLE FOR SMALL STREAMS

Tackle for small-stream fly fishing is pretty straightforward, although there is plenty of room for a few personal quirks. Brushy, overgrown streams make short fly rods more practical. I like a $7^1/_2$-foot or 7-foot, 9-inch rod for average small-stream work. Rods this length are long enough to dap a fly where necessary and hold fly line off the water to prevent drag, but short enough to maneuver in the close confines of your average small streams. Very tight, overgrown, or exceptionally small streams may require a rod as short as 6 feet.

If you like fishing very light lines, small-stream work is an ideal place for 0-weight to 2-weight rods, although personally I still prefer a 3-weight or 4-weight for general small-stream applications. I also like the versatility of a bamboo rod, but slower-action graphite or fiberglass rods also make decent small-stream fishing tools. Be aware that most of your casts will be very short, so you either want a rod that loads quickly or you should be prepared to make up for the lack of loading by modifying your casting style. Some small-stream anglers cut a standard length fly line in half and overline their small-stream graphite rod by as much as two or three line weights to get it to load more quickly. You can get a similar effect without overlining if you use a slower action fly rod.

I start off with a 6-foot to $7^1/2$-foot leader tapered to a 4X tippet for typical riffle, glide, plunge pool, pocketwater type small-stream conditions. If I run into slower-moving meadow water conditions or beaver ponds, I carry 4X to 6X leader material that allows me to lengthen and lighten the tippet if necessary.

You really don't need more than a single box of flies to fish most small streams. My box has the standard attractor and searcher dry-fly patterns such as the Royal Coachman, Royal Coachman Trude, Rio Grande King Trude, grasshoppers, Parachute Hare's Ears, Stimulators, Elk Hair Caddis, Adams, and Lime Trudes in sizes varying from 16 to 12. In addition I include a few smaller-sized

flies, which will sometimes save the day when nothing else works. I carry general-purpose weighted or beadhead nymphs such as the Gold-Ribbed Hare's Ear, Prince, Brassie, and Pheasant Tail to be used as droppers behind the dry flies. Finally, I never leave home without a few ant and beetle patterns, which can be killers on small streams. If you have trouble seeing them, simply trail them behind a more visible dry-fly pattern in the same way you would trail a nymph pattern.

There is an elusive angling quality that you'll want to fine-tune as a backcountry small-stream fly fisher. It's best described as a kind of all-around awareness or presence. For example, you might have lacked awareness the first time you didn't check behind you to see if you could make a backcast or the first time you did check behind you and

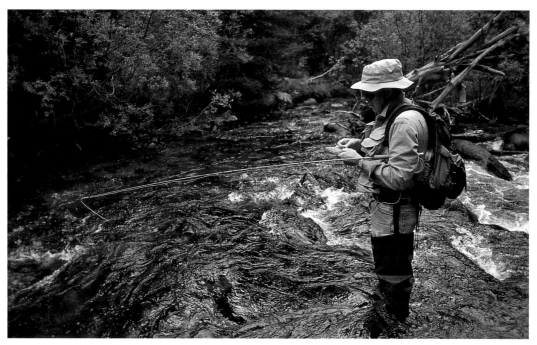

The slower action and versatility of a bamboo fly rod makes it ideal for fishing small streams.

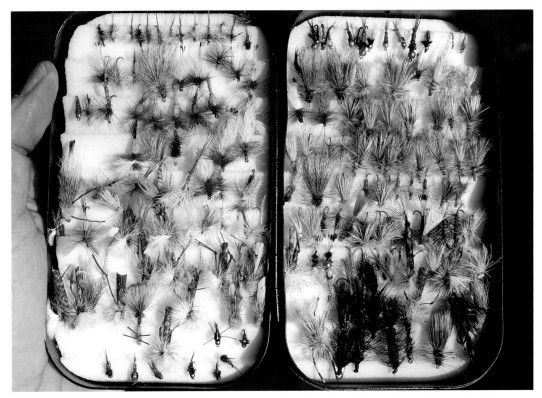

The organized chaos of a small-stream fly box is a wonderful thing. The trick is to have a few copies of a variety of different fly patterns that cover a range of sizes, rather than carrying a large number of duplicates of any single pattern.

successfully completed one cast and then changed the plane of your next cast just a smidgen and got hung up in the trees. Other common breakdowns in awareness result in streakers busting out far upstream or missed opportunities because all you saw was the sweet plunge pool upstream and spooked a 12-inch cutt in the eight inches of water you were crashing through to get to it. The list goes on. I'll just say the very best small-stream anglers I know are aware, patient, and observant. They are the anglers that take the time to see the small-stream opportunities that the rest of us don't.

Sooner or later, you'll find out if you're really cut out to be a backcountry small-stream angler. That means you'll find yourself delighted by things like the Small Stream Stress Index (SSSI) that some friends of mine put together. They classified backcountry small streams on a one to five scale. A number one was a stream that was fairly open where you had reasonable odds of making a successful backcast without getting hung up. A number five was a briar patch of a stream where backcasts were absolutely impossible and you had to dap the fly or sneak upstream and feed line out to drift the fly downstream to its target. The frustration level was so high on number fives that you took an old fly rod along so when you broke it over your knee at least you hadn't wrecked your favorite fishing tool.

The key is to learn to take the little small-stream frustrations in stride, and if you do, things will begin to fall into place. You unconsciously check behind you before every cast, you travel light, you are quiet, and eventually the day comes when you wonder what's next. That's when you begin to think maybe, just maybe, there could be some larger trout that you're missing.

CATCHING LARGER SMALL-STREAM TROUT

I learned a new trick on a small stream that I'd fished for years. The stream was characterized by plunge pools, fast pocketwater, gravel-bottomed shallows, and an occasional stretch of flat, gliding water where the gradient flattened out into a pool. I'd decided to take a break next to a narrow twenty-foot-long pool and wait for my fishing partner, who was somewhere downstream. I sat up against a tree and passed the time by watching the main current push into the pool and glide along the opposite bank. I'd fished this pool hundreds of times. It was one of those places that always got my attention. And I'd done well there picking off the occasional above-average trout and plenty of smaller fish.

After about twenty minutes of observation, I saw one of the subtlest rises I've ever seen. It was right up against the opposite bank. After a few minutes, I saw the rise again. It was the kind of rise larger spring creek trout make—not the exaggerated

small-stream trout rise I was used to. I slowly lowered my fly rod from where it was leaning up against a tree, lengthened the tippet a few feet, and changed to a smaller, parachute-style dry fly. I then made my way on my hands and knees to a downstream-and-across casting position. I checked for backcast clearance, visualized exactly where I wanted my fly to land, held my breath, and threaded a couple of backcasts through the trees. The fly landed pretty close to where I wanted it to be. It bumped along the opposite bank for a foot or so before the trout took it. I hooked up and landed a 15-inch cutthroat trout! I'd fished this pool diligently every summer for the past eight years and never caught a trout larger than 11 inches. The largest trout I'd ever caught anywhere in the stream was about 12 inches.

I could have just discounted it as right-place-at-the-right-time luck, but I decided to test an idea. I'd noticed several years before how frightened trout often streaked out upstream from me, and I had learned to be more careful on my approach. The stealthier approach in itself had resulted in some larger-than-average-size fish, but even my most careful approaches on some water still produced streakers. It was only when I'd actually sat quietly by the water without any movement for twenty minutes that I'd caught a surprisingly large trout. Up until then, I'd always figured the streakers were just part of the equation, and there were still plenty of other trout to catch. I hadn't considered that some of those extra-wary fish that streaked to cover upstream of me might be larger than average or maybe even larger than any trout I'd ever caught from the stream.

When your stealthiest approach still spooks fish, the only alternative may be to take a seat and just observe the water until you see signs of activity. Your patience might well be rewarded by a larger-than-average trout.

I decided that a careful, stealthy approach wasn't going to be enough to totally solve the streaker problem. The only solution was to not move at all for a while, especially when I came to water that I thought might hold a larger fish. Now when I see any water that has that kind of potential, I very quietly find a spot to sit where I can be in a casting position with minimal disturbance. I then watch the water for fifteen to thirty minutes. It's a habit that's paid off with some trout that were larger than any I'd ever expected to catch. The key is to wait as long as you can stand it while observing the water and then approach your casting position as unobtrusively as possible. For me this means

going on all fours or crouching very low and not getting into the water. I make all my casts from the bank. Finally, I make my first cast my best cast.

There are a few other tricks you can use to improve your chances for larger trout on small streams. One is to always pay attention to any hatch. Where I live, we get a size 12 Red Quill hatch on many of our small streams. It brings all the trout to the surface. I've fished a section of water before the hatch and then gone back through that same stretch during the hatch and caught twice as many trout. Some of these fish are always larger than average. The fact is that many upland streams don't have a lot of significant hatches, but when they do, be ready for some great fishing. You probably won't even have to closely match the naturals because the trout will really be keyed to the action, but I still carry a few matches for the common small-stream hatches in my area just in case they get picky.

In addition to flies that match specific local hatches, you should always have some smaller ant, beetle, and grasshopper patterns. I seldom find that larger small-stream trout key specifically to any particular terrestrial pattern, but for reasons that are unclear to me, using a smaller-size terrestrial sometimes produces surprising results.

USING TOPOGRAPHICAL MAPS TO FIND SMALL STREAMS

Your best shot at larger trout will always be on familiar small streams, but you can come up with some ideas about unknown small streams by studying topographic maps. Traditionally, most fly fishers depend on the work of others to find good small streams. A fishing buddy might take you to his favorite small stream if you promise to keep the location secret. It's a generous gesture, but it always seems like somehow the word gets out. Another approach is to try to gain a local resident's confidence and then ask where the good small streams are. Although a tip from a

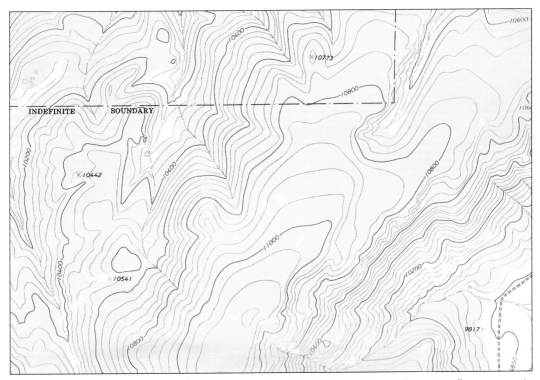

A 7.5-minute series topographic map features contour lines. The distance between the contour lines represents a 40-foot vertical increase or decrease in elevation. A darker brown contour line with the elevation indicated occurs every five contour lines.

local does pan out once in a while, it more often results in some kind of ridiculous wild-goose chase that has the whole community laughing through most of the winter.

Eventually it becomes clear that you're going to have to find your own small-stream fishing. For some that means putting the shoe leather to the trail and fishing any small stream they come across that looks good. Of course, on-the-ground exploration is ultimately the only way you'll be able to determine the angling potential of a small stream, but you can also waste a lot of time and energy if all you're doing is randomly sampling streams.

You can focus your search for fishable small streams by conducting a map study of the areas that you believe have potential before you check them out on the ground. For many years, I began my map searches with a U.S. Forest Service map. This large-scale map (typically about 1:126,000) is useful because it shows public and private land, special regulation areas (wilderness, roadless areas, etc.), trails, Forest Service access roads, and most important, rivers and streams. What the Forest Service map can't tell you is the lay of the land.

You need a 7.5-minute series (1:24,000 scale) map, commonly known as a topographic or topo map to determine that because topos include contour lines. The brown contour lines can be used to determine elevation and percent slope of any location on the map. The distance between the contour lines represents a forty-foot vertical increase or decrease in elevation. A darker brown contour line with the elevation occurs every five contour lines. So if you follow one of the darker contour lines, you will

eventually come to a figure, say 6,600 feet, for example. There will be four lighter colored brown lines (a 200-foot vertical change in elevation) between it and the next darker brown contour line, which is either 6,400 feet or 6,800, feet, depending on whether you looked upslope or downslope.

The Forest Service and topo map system works fine, but it's cumbersome and expensive. You may need as many as four or five topos just to figure out if it's worth hiking into a drainage. Fortunately that changed when computer-based topo map programs became available. Now it's as easy as a few mouse clicks to go to a large-scale 1:500,000 map that shows public and private land boundaries and then from there go to a 1:100,000 scale map with larger interval contour lines for an overview of the landscape. Finally, you can bring up a 1:24,000 scale topographic map for a detailed look at the area. Most map programs can be used to plot waypoints into a GPS unit, and some will allow you to segue directly to an Internet site with a satellite photo of your specific area of interest. All of the programs can print a copy of the topo map to guide you to your targeted destination.

Whether you use paper maps or a computer program, you will need to determine what characteristics make the angling potential of one stream better than another. Stream slope is usually the most critical factor. A very steep stream slope often indicates a steady downstream cascade of water, meaning there will be fewer of the pockets and pools of deeper water that are crucial holding and feeding areas for trout. A stream with a less severe slope has a better chance of providing the necessary habitat for trout.

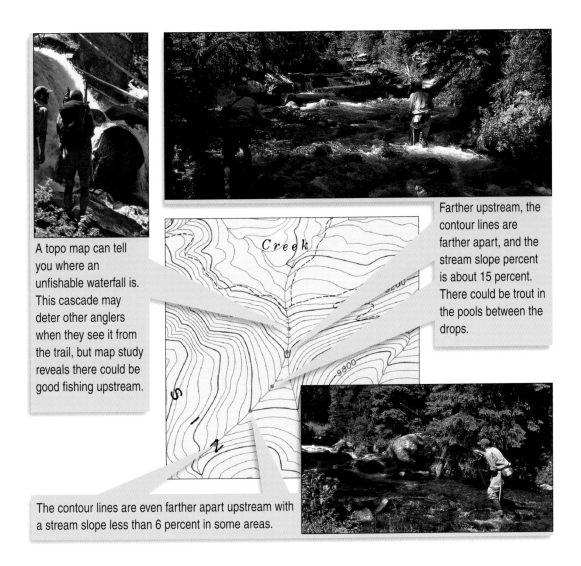

A topo map can tell you where an unfishable waterfall is. This cascade may deter other anglers when they see it from the trail, but map study reveals there could be good fishing upstream.

Farther upstream, the contour lines are farther apart, and the stream slope percent is about 15 percent. There could be trout in the pools between the drops.

The contour lines are even farther apart upstream with a stream slope less than 6 percent in some areas.

You can measure the stream slope percent by counting the number of contour lines that cross the stream over a specific distance. Most computer map programs have a function that will measure that distance in miles. You'll have to convert the miles into feet (multiply by 5,280 feet) and then divide that figure into the change in the elevation. The change in elevation is the number of con-

tour lines counted in the specified distance multiplied by 40 feet.

I've learned over the years that a stream slope of 15 percent or less holds good angling possibilities; 10 percent slope or less is prime. Once in a while, a stream slope as high as 20 or even 25 percent can support trout due to a unique stream characteristic such as a drop-and-pool structure.

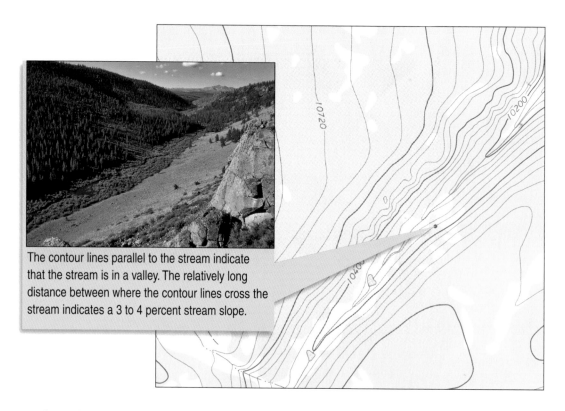

The contour lines parallel to the stream indicate that the stream is in a valley. The relatively long distance between where the contour lines cross the stream indicates a 3 to 4 percent stream slope.

If you don't want to do the math, you can get a pretty good qualitative idea of a stream's potential by just looking at how close together the contour lines are as you follow the stream course. As a general rule, the farther apart they are the greater the chance for good trout habitat. You should also pay attention to the width of the floodplain. Typically a floodplain is pretty flat. The map may actually show a meandering stream course in broader floodplains. This could indicate a meadow environment with a less severe stream slope that means good holding water and undercut banks, or it might be a willow-choked flat that could still provide difficult, but rewarding, angling. A narrow floodplain with a stream slope between 6 percent and 15 percent usually indicates a riffle-and-pool or drop-and-pool stream structure that may provide excellent pocketwater fishing.

You should also study the subtleties of how the stream moves through the terrain during the map survey. A stream can appear quite rugged when viewed as a whole, but more detailed study may reveal a short eighth or sixteenth of a mile section that holds real promise. These areas are often hidden in the overall ruggedness of the terrain and overlooked by anglers.

There are some other factors to consider during the map survey. As a rule, the farther a stream is from a road the better—any water that's more than an hour-long hike probably won't receive much pressure. You should also look at stream access. A maintained trail means there will probably be

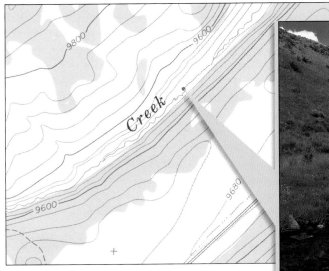

The narrow floodplain indicates that this stream will probably have some bends and curves here and there but few full-blown meanders, even though the stream slope is 2 to 3 percent.

more people in the vicinity of the stream, but they won't necessarily be fishing. If no trail to the stream is visible, determine a safe way to get to it and program waypoints for your GPS navigating tool. When you go into the field be sure to bring the topo map, a compass, and your GPS tool and know how to use them. You should also leave word with a responsible party about where you are going and when you plan to return.

Another terrain feature to look for is the high lakes that feed small streams. These headwater high lakes offer a lot of fishing potential, but they are also magnets that provide a real draw for every fisherman who looks at a map. Once again, the farther the hike to the lake the better the odds are that you'll have it to yourself, but always assume

you'll see other fishermen. An alternative plan is to carefully examine the outlet stream from the lake. These streams often receive little pressure from lake fishermen and have excellent angling potential.

Beaver ponds almost always attract back-country anglers' attention because they hold the potential for larger fish. When you examine them on a topo map be aware that the information could be quite a few years old. The beaver ponds shown on the map could literally be dried up. The ponds indicated on any topo map are best taken to mean that beavers have inhabited the area and there may still be some viable older ponds or hopefully a few new ponds, but remember what's on the map and what you find when you hike there could be quite different. Up-

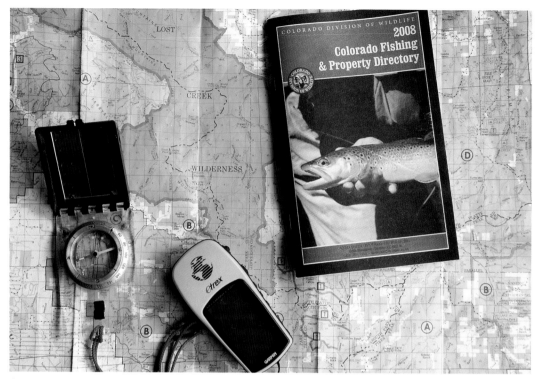

A map, compass, and GPS navigating tool—and the ability to use them—can help you safely get to out-of-the-way small streams. Don't forget to check for any special fishing regulations that might apply to the backcountry streams you're heading to.

to-date satellite photos will give you a more reliable idea of the condition of the ponds.

Ultimately, any map survey can only go so far. At some point you must decide which small streams or beaver-pond systems you think offer the best potential and then lace up your boots and go check out your hunches.

FISHING BEAVER PONDS

In the hierarchy of trout water, beaver ponds are the most ephemeral. The beavers come, build their dams, the water backs up, and nutrients begin to pool in the pond. Everything grows, including the trout. With every spring runoff and every summer afternoon

thunderstorm, silt pours into the pond along with the water, and the beaver pond begins the process of filling in. The aquatic vegetation that has supported the insects that have supported the trout begins to disappear. The pond gets shallow. The larger trout are the first to move on. The smaller brookies or cutts will try to inhabit the pond to the end. Eventually the beavers move upstream and start over. They build a new dam. A new pond forms, and the cycle begins anew.

I have seen good beaver ponds that supported footlong brook trout come and go in less than a decade. I've seen beaver ponds that held big cutthroat trout blown out by

A beaver pond is in a constant state of change. Dated topographical maps may not represent the current condition of the ponds. An up-to-date satellite photo is a more reliable source of current information.

spring runoff and never rebuilt. And I know places that once held shallow beaver ponds that are now meadows. But every beaver pond follows its own destiny. Some are blessed. They are deep with strong, oxygen-bearing water flows that prevent winterkill. And the aspen and willows that sustain the beavers are so abundant that they stay on working the ponds, maintaining and creating trout habitat. And the beaver-pond system flourishes. Legendary trout grow. The pond becomes the thing that backcountry anglers dream about.

Beaver ponds and the trout they hold are among the closest secrets that anglers keep. On the surface, the reasons seem obvious—beaver ponds and beaver-pond trout are finite entities. They might be fished out or abused. Paradise might be lost. The most tightly kept secrets are the places where you are apt to find the very best beaver-pond fishing. In the Rocky Mountains where I live, they are remote, pristine, and beautiful. Finding them requires hard exploratory work and unswerving faith. You must know that the cosmic beaver pond is out there, or you'll never find it. And when you do, it will quiet you because above and beyond the trout and the water there will be the country you find yourself in. You'll want to protect that solitude, and that quiet, and that beauty.

A casting position below a beaver pond has a number of advantages—the dam covers your approach and the stream below the dam provides a casting lane for your backcast.

I can honestly say that the majority of the beaver ponds I've fished over the years have yielded what most anglers would consider small trout. Where I live, you expect to find brook trout or cutthroat trout in most beaver ponds, but you might also find brown trout or rainbow trout. I have fished some beaver-pond systems where I've caught all four major trout species. Other beaver ponds may hold exotics such as golden trout or grayling. The bottom line is that a healthy beaver-pond system is so rich that it can support all kinds of life.

It's best to use a systems approach when fly-fishing beaver ponds. Beavers seldom build just one pond. You'll find that the ponds often tend to work their way in series

up a stream with the older ponds downstream and the newer ponds up the stream. Rather than looking at each pond individually, I look at all the ponds and the streams and marsh that interconnect them as one whole system. In mountainous country, I plan my approach to include a ridge or hilltop that will overlook the ponds. From a higher vantage point, it's easy to see how the whole system fits together.

When I make my overview of the ponds, I try to determine how many there are and note where any larger or deeper ponds are located. It's helpful to identify an unmistakable landmark, such as a particularly tall or crooked tree, to help guide you to the various ponds once you've entered the heavy vegetation that surrounds many beaver ponds. I also look for ways to approach the ponds that will provide casting lanes in the willows. I always study the connector streams between beaver ponds. Some of the largest trout I've caught in beaver-pond systems have come from the undercut banks along the often narrow and deep connector streams. Finally, I use compact binoculars and Polaroid sunglasses to locate trout, which are often visible from a distance in the very clear water.

Once I've done my reconnaissance work, I typically approach the pond system from the downstream side unless I've located a specific pond that just looks too good to resist. I try to visit any fishable beaver pond and the interconnecting streams, but I do prioritize my time on the water to make sure

I get to the larger and deeper ponds, which usually hold more promise for larger trout.

An easy and effective approach to a beaver pond is to wade up the stream below it to the dam. Once I'm directly below the dam and assuming it's not too tall to see over, I look for rising trout or any fish that might be working under the water's surface. Once I've located the trout, I cast to them from below the dam. This is advantageous for several reasons. First, wading into casting position in the stream below the dam covers your approach. If you wade carefully, it's very quiet. Also, when you position yourself below the dam, the stream provides a perfect casting lane for your backcast.

If I don't see rising trout when I approach from below the dam, I still use a dry fly to

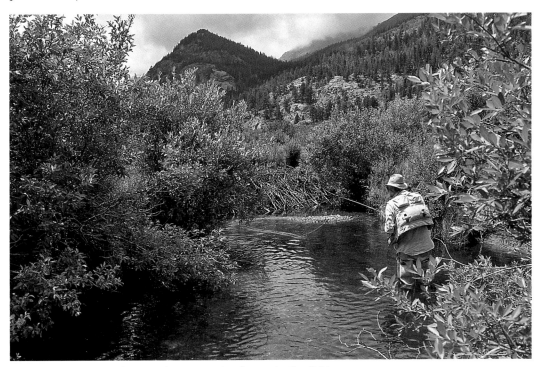

The connector streams between beaver ponds offer productive fishing.

explore the deep, dam end of the pond. Like small-stream trout, beaver-pond trout tend to be opportunistic and will often take a dry fly even when there are no naturals on the surface. The best tactic is to cast into shady areas under the willows. Leave the dry fly on the water's surface until any disturbance from the presentation has dissipated, and then twitch the fly. The result is often a crashing strike.

Another option is to switch to some sort of wet fly or nymph. The Partridge and Orange, a simple Hare's Ear wet fly, a small olive damselfly nymph imitation, or a Zug Bug are great searcher patterns. I try to systematically work all the water within my casting range when using either wets or dry flies from a below-the-dam casting position.

Once I've worked the pond from below the dam, I get up on top of it and extend my casts to cover more water. When fishing dry flies, I pay special attention, once again, to shady areas, riseforms, and structure where trout might be looking up from just under the water's surface. I work weighted wets or streamers in these same areas and in the deeper main channel that is discernible in many beaver ponds. Larger trout often lurk in the dark channel water. Expect to lose a few flies when you work them among the sticks and structure along the bottom of the beaver pond.

When I've covered everything within reach from the dam end of the pond, I fish my way around to the inlet. Where possible I try to weave a backcast through pond-side vegetation, but in many cases you'll need to use roll casts or steeple casts. The inlet to a beaver pond can provide good fishing. I look for rising trout or trout holding in the flow taking nymphs. Inlets can be particu-larly productive during spring or fall spawning runs.

You might have a less than perfect day on the beaver ponds if you buy into the idea that beaver-pond trout are dumb. The smaller fish may readily accept your offerings, but larger beaver-pond trout can be crafty. If you think about it, they have some distinct advantages. Beaver-pond water is usually crystal clear, and on a calm day *any* size tippet looks like a rope being dropped on the water. If you crash around in willows that surround a pond, it's likely that your presence will be telegraphed to the more wary trout. Footfalls in marshy terrain will also alert the trout to your presence. Just the momentary passing of your shadow over the water's surface will spook even the smaller fish.

The key is to assume a monster trout is finning quietly near the surface on every beaver pond. Make your approach accordingly. Pay special attention to your first look at the water. Keep a low profile. Use the vegetation to break up your silhouette, and make sure your fly rod isn't silhouetted against the sky when casting. Remember that your first casts will probably be the most important in terms of the larger fish. Once you've made those first few casts, the value of extreme stealth will diminish. Also note that the larger trout may be more active and easier to approach during the low-light hours of the early morning and evening.

Beaver-pond trout, with the exception of heavily fished ponds, aren't usually selective feeders, but it's important for fly fishers to note the unique beaver-pond environment and carry flies that complement it. I have found over the years that my standard small-stream fly box is also a good basic fly selection for beaver-pond trout, but I do add a few additional flies. I like to have weighted Hare's Ear soft hackles and several Sylvester Nemes–style traditional partridge hackle wets in size 12 to 16. I don't always carry streamers when I know I'll just be fishing small streams, but I make a point to have a selection in my fly box when I'll be fishing beaver ponds. I include olive and black Woolly Buggers, Mickey Finns, a few small Zonkers, and a brown or olive Marabou Leech. Patterns with red, orange, and yellow seem to be especially attractive to brook trout and cutthroats. I like smaller streamers from size 12 to size 6. Finally, be sure to throw in a few smaller, general-purpose dry flies such as a size 20 Adams Parachute, CDC Dun, or Griffith's Gnat just in case the trout get selective to the small stuff that sometimes hatches from the stillwaters of a beaver pond.

I still strive to limit my flies to a single box. The important thing is to have a variety of pattern types and sizes rather than lots of copies of any single fly.

Targeting Larger Beaver-Pond Trout

As you gain more beaver-pond fishing experience, you'll begin to notice that big-trout beaver ponds tend to have certain characteristics in common. Most are isolated and receive low to moderate fishing pressure. Fishery biologists will tell you that they are usually more than a half-acre in size, eight feet deep or deeper, and have a good year-round source of water flowing into them. If the pond holds brook trout, usually some factor, such as lack of spawning gravel, limits the uncontrolled growth of the population.

Some of these larger beaver-pond trout may simply attack the same large dry fly that

Larger, deeper beaver ponds with a good year-round source of water coming into them are most likely to produce the trophy-size beaver pond trout.

The greatest small-stream thrill is to catch a native trout in a backcountry drainage where its ancestors have finned the same waters for countless generations.

worked on the smaller trout. Others may succumb to a beadhead nymph trailed behind a dry fly. These are lucky trout. Catching them basically comes down to being in the right place at the right time.

But you can increase your chances of landing larger beaver-pond trout. Of course, stealth is crucial. If possible, approach the pond by way of the stream below the dam to avoid detection. I like to fish small

streamers when I'm targeting larger beaver-pond trout. Although casting from a position below the dam does hide your silhouette and makes for easier casting, you may spook trout when the streamer hits the glassy surface of the beaver pond. This is especially true when conditions are calm or the sun is high overhead. A careful approach from the inlet side of the beaver pond will allow you to use a series of S curves in the line to feed the streamer downstream to the sweet spots in the channel. If there are too many obstacles in the channel, consider feeding a dry fly with a beadhead dropper downstream through the channel.

As seductive as beaver ponds are, they do tend to draw the attention of backcountry fishermen. Your best chance to catch larger trout will be early in the season before the ponds have been hammered by other fishermen, or find ponds located in remote locales that receive little pressure.

Finding and fishing productive backcountry small streams and beaver ponds is sweet medicine. I can't say that I've found a lot of undiscovered hot spots over the years, but I have come across a few isolated or remote sections of water that I believe have remained essentially unfished. Thirty years ago when I first started poring over topo maps to find dreamy small streams or hidden beaver ponds, I pretty much had my eyes focused on the prize. And there have been a few. But, ultimately, if you are like me, you'll probably find that as gratifying as it is to land a trophy beaver-pond trout or a small-stream giant, it's the hunt and the wild places that keep you coming back. Nowadays I still hope to find a hidden gem, but it is the journey and discovery I enjoy the most.

CHAPTER 8

Oddities

Dry flies that sink, spiders, and triggers

It's hard to complain about early July in Colorado's South Park. The South Platte River's Tricos are really kicking in by then, and the trout are tipping up and sipping. I try to pack a lot of guide trips in during that time because I like helping fly fishermen understand how powerful a tiny fly can be. Of course, when it comes to Tricos you need to add a nice portion of patience to the mix too. It always amazes me how many times you can stick a cast just right and everything seemingly unfolds perfectly, but the trout still doesn't take the fly. The only other surface event that approaches this kind of disregard on the trout's part is when they are sipping midge pupae from the surface film.

If you've been around me at all, you will have heard what I'm going to say next about Tricos. I'm going to ask you how many times you have hooked up on a fish when you couldn't see your spent spinner imita-

tion on the water's surface. And you're going to reply that it has happened a lot, but you figure the fly is so small and sits down so low into the surface film that you're lucky if you see it 50 percent of the time. Finally you'll admit that a lot of your hookups actually occur when you feel a tug through the line or when you go to pick up the fly line for the next cast and you realize you have a fish on! That, of course, is when I chime in and say, "Has it ever occurred to you that your fly may have sunk an inch or two below the surface? It's really a pretty sparse tie, and it probably wouldn't take much for it to break the surface film and sink. You have to figure the odds are good that those polypropylene or Antron wings aren't going to buoy it back up to the surface either."

The real clincher is when I mention that the natural spinners that have fallen spent to the water's surface are dead and do

Sometimes a Trico spent spinner imitation that is designed to float actually works better when it sinks.

eventually sink if a trout doesn't eat them first, and that the trout, and especially the larger trout, actually seek out those spent spinners that have sunk below the surface. How can they lose? They can eat as many of them as they could on the surface *and* not show themselves to predators. It's a great opportunity. And opportunity is the most important word you'll hear in my entire spiel. Even in the most demanding, do-everything-perfect, match-the-hatch situations, you will still find that trout are opportunists. And when that spinner imitation you're fishing sinks, it's a real opportunity for that trout to get what it wants with less risk.

I have another related story from July that you should hear. I once taught fly fishing

A spent Trico spinner will eventually sink if a trout doesn't eat it first.

at an outdoor guide school in Colorado. I liked it because most of my students weren't cut from the same cloth as the fly-fishing guides you see on the river nowadays. These students had come to the school to take other courses such as wilderness horsemanship, horse packing, judging trophy big-game animals, survival, and outfitting. The weeklong fly-fishing guide school was more of an afterthought. Most of my students realized they wouldn't become hotshot spring-creek fly-fishing guides, but they were hoping they might be able to extend their big-game hunting season by packing fly fishermen up into the wilderness during the summer months. As their teacher, I basically tried to get them thinking and speaking like fly fishers. We started with a morning of fly-casting instruction on the grass and then went fly fishing for five days. During that time, I tried to teach them basic fly-fishing techniques and impart a little of the philosophy that I thought made fly fishing different from other kinds of sport fishing.

We spent our first full day on the South Platte River learning the ins and outs of short-line dead-drift nymphing. It was the basic stuff, you know the drill—put just enough weight on the leader to get a two-fly rig to the bottom and then allow it to bounce downstream in a natural fashion. I introduced them to strike indicators, but only after we'd spent some time nymphing without one. I stressed that they had the best chance for solid hookups if they fished as short a line as they could. By the end of the day, everyone had gotten at least a few strikes and most of them had landed and released a trout or two.

We spent our next day on the river learning dry-fly basics. My fly of choice for their first dry-fly lesson was a grasshopper pattern. There were actually some real hoppers around since it was July, but more important, it was a nice-sized fly that the students could see when they were practicing their mends and drag-free drifts.

The dry-fly day with hoppers dovetailed nicely into the following day's lesson when we headed down to the Arkansas River to learn the popular hopper-dropper technique where a beadhead or weighted nymph is trailed behind a grasshopper pattern. The hopper provides the buoyancy to suspend the nymph imitation in the water column and also acts as a strike indicator when a trout takes the nymph. The match-the-hatch/attractor nature of the hopper in this configuration also has the added clout of attracting a fair number of strikes on its own. The hopper-dropper lesson was intended to bring the nymphing and dry-fly lessons full circle. It would also demonstrate that it was possible to suspend a weighted subsurface fly imitation in the water column rather than bounce it along the stream bottom and still get strikes.

After we had gone over the rig, I sent the students out on the water to give it a try. I later walked upstream behind them and observed. That's when one of them, who had a fish on, showed me a new trick. After he landed the chunky rainbow trout, he said he'd caught two other trout and released them. I noticed then that he was fishing a dead-drift nymphing rig with a strike indicator and weight on the leader. The grasshopper pattern was tied to the tippet about eight inches below the weight.

"That doesn't look like a hopper and dropper rig to me," I said.

"I know, but I did so well dead-drift nymphing the other day I just thought I'd try this," he replied.

When I surveyed the other students, I found that he'd caught more fish and larger fish than anyone else. That's when it occurred to me that, with the exception of the strike indicator, he had been fishing the hopper

A grasshopper is a terrestrial, and if the trout don't get to it pretty quickly when it lands on the water, it will sink.

imitation exactly the way I fished live hoppers when I was a kid, and whether or not he knew it, his strategy made good sense. A grasshopper is a terrestrial, and if a trout doesn't get to it pretty quickly when it lands on the water, it will eventually sink. The odds are that for every few live hoppers that a trout takes on the surface, it's probably taking at least that many under the surface.

DRY FLIES THAT SINK

I'd thought about drowning Trico spinner imitations before, but I'd never really considered that other dry flies that happen to sink might be just as effective. I've done some research since then and found that grasshopper patterns that are designed to sink have been around for decades. Some of them replace the ubiquitous deer-hair hopper head with a wool head that just speeds up how quickly the fly becomes waterlogged and sinks. Mike

Lawson's Wet Hopper incorporates a mottled partridge hackle and red fox squirrel wing, which tends to absorb water to sink the fly.

More recently, Eric Ishiwata's Busted Hopper uses soft, water-absorbing materials and a hefty black tungsten bead. It imitates a long-dead hopper that's gotten beaten up by the current, has sunk, and is tumbling along the stream bottom. When dead-drifted using standard nymphing techniques in deeper holes and along undercut banks, the fly has a reputation for getting the attention of larger trout. Rick Takahashi's Drowned Hopper is a variation of his friend Ishiwata's Busted Hopper that is designed for use with a dry-fly/dropper rig. The pattern also employs wet-fly-type materials and an olive-colored brass bead.

Other tiers simply retain the well-known deer-hair head hopper design but add weight to the fly's body, which creates a kind

ISHIWATA'S BUSTED HOPPER

Hook:	Tiemco 5262, size 10–14; or Dai-Riki 710
Bead:	2.8 mm black or copper tungsten
Thread:	Yellow 8/0 Uni
Tail:	Red hackle fibers tied short
Abdomen:	Aussie possum dubbing
Rib:	Copper Ultra Wire, Brassie size
Wing:	Olive Pheasant tail scrapes
Legs:	Brown hen hackle feathers
Thorax:	Aussie possum dubbing (optional turkey quill)
Collar:	Partridge

TAKAHASHI'S DROWNED HOPPER #1

Hook:	Tiemco 2457, size 8–12 or Dai-Riki 135
Bead:	Olive Spirit River or Umpqua brass bead
Thread:	Olive dun 6/0 Uni-Thread
Tail:	Red hackle fibers tied short
Abdomen:	Strip of quarter-inch latex colored with a tan marker
Underwing:	Natural CDC fibers
Wing:	Montana Fly Company mottled brown wing material
Overwing:	Coq de Leon dark pardo feather fibers
Legs:	Olive Metz Hopper Legs
Hackle:	Olive Whiting Farms Brahma hen hackle
Thorax:	Dark Olive Crawdub dubbing
Collar:	Peacock Ice Dub

Most grasshopper patterns are designed as dry flies, but they will also catch trout if they are fished below the surface.

good imitation of a drowned hopper with its wings swept back. And, of course, you can always go the route my guide school student did—just fish a standard deer-hair head hopper with a standard weight-on-the-leader dead-drift nymphing rig. The imitation is good, and the buoyancy of the deer hair probably activates the fly even more.

Once the idea registers that you can drown a hopper imitation, it's pretty much a no-brainer that any terrestrial imitation will catch trout below the surface. I now have ants and beetles in my fly box that I've tied specifically to sink, although less fastidious anglers could easily get away with using a standard dry-fly version of either one in a dead-drift nymphing rig. As it turns out, a lot of the ant and beetle patterns that we used before foam revolutionized how these patterns are tied would sink after you fished them for a while. I remember getting strikes on black deer-hair beetles that sunk and, in particular, the lacquered-thread ant patterns that were popular in the 1970s.

The idea of sinking dry flies doesn't have to stop with terrestrials. We've seen what a drowned Trico spinner can do and for that matter any spent spinner pattern. A good strategy is to fish a spent spinner imitation on the surface first, but if it doesn't work, don't forget to drown it. I've caught trout by drowning spent spinners during all sorts of mayfly hatch events. It doesn't necessarily have to be during the spinnerfall either. One of my secret weapons when I'm having trouble catching fish during a dun emergence is to switch to a spent spinner imitation that matches the dun, and if it doesn't work on top, I pull it under the surface and see what happens.

of neutral density, causing it to hang in the water column. If you have ever dead-drifted a weighted Muddler Minnow, this neutral density hopper rendition immediately makes you wonder what the trout might have been taking the Muddler for. Actually, among all its other attributes, the Muddler is a pretty

Deer-hair beetle imitations tend to sink after they have been fished for a while.

The Elk Hair Caddis is sometimes effective when pulled under the water's surface and fished on a tight line like a wet fly.

The lacquered-thread ant patterns popular in the 1970s were almost more effective when they sank an inch or two below the surface than when they were fished as dry flies.

A final thought to consider is that any dry fly ought to be fair game for drowning if it isn't working the way it's supposed to (i.e., catching trout) on the surface. I first learned this when I was fishing an Elk Hair Caddis. At the end of the drift I allowed the fly to swing and skitter on the surface in hopes of attracting a strike. Somewhere along the way I got a little lazy and allowed the current to pull the fly under and immediately got a strike. Needless to say, I incorporated that into my presentation and started catching trout.

A similar occurrence was the basis of a story I related in my book, *Fishing Small Flies*, where I found that pulling an Elk Hair Caddis under the surface on the swing during a Pale Morning Dun hatch often resulted in a strike. Explanations about why that worked are sketchy, but it might be that

Pale Morning Duns, along with some *Heptagenia* nymphs, emerge from the nymphal shuck on the way to the surface during which time their wings are folded back along the sides of the body. A drowned Elk Hair Caddis would create a silhouette similar to that. Of course, it might also be that the trout are on the feed and simply taking the fly as an attractor. However, I now am in the habit of pulling any dry fly under and letting it swing at the end of the drift if the trout aren't taking it on the surface. The practice doesn't always elicit strikes, and it can wreck a good dry fly. Sometimes it even puts the trout down. But it does work at times and has been the impetus necessary to induce me to switch from a dry fly pulled under the surface to a soft-hackle fly fished on a tight line. That switch has often resulted in great success.

SPIDERS

I think most of the fly fishers in my generation have had a fling or two with spider flies. The fly itself is nothing more that than a few very long dry-fly hackles wrapped around a short-shank fine wire hook. I don't even know how these quirky flies managed to get into our collective fly-fishing consciousness in the 1970s. By then the mainstream was pretty much a match-the-hatch, selective trout, and there-has-to-be-a-scientific-solution-to-catching-every-feeding-trout kind of techno world. And that was alright because it seemed like we were all catching more trout.

But in the midst of it all there was the spider. You never saw it for sale in any fly shops, yet somehow everybody knew about it. It was the kind of fly that you kept a copy or two of in your fly box, and when nothing was happening at high noon somebody would say, "You might tie on a spider. I saw a few crane flies earlier." The reference to crane flies came mostly out of the current match-the-hatch logic because the spider, which was designed to dance, skate, and skitter over the water's surface, looked like a crane fly if you fished it right. Other match-the-hatch theories pegged it as an imitation of any large mayfly adult dancing over the water's surface. Some fly fishers simply thought the oversize hackle represented the whir of action that a caddisfly's wings made as it navigated over the water's surface and dipped down to deposit its eggs.

Edward R. Hewitt is credited with modifying what was generally known in the 1920s as a spider dry fly into the spider we know today. I'm not sure that he really considered what his Neversink Skater Fly

imitated. By all accounts Hewitt simply eliminated the original spider's tail and a few other extraneous parts and settled on tying two extra-long stiff rooster spade hackles to a fine wire, short-shank size 16 hook. The genius of the fly was the way it was tied. Hewitt tied the rear hackle with the shiny side toward the hook bend and the forward hackle with the shiny side toward the hook eye. When he wrapped hackles that were tied in that way, the concave sides faced each other. That meant the tips would come together, allowing the fly to literally dance across the water on single points rather than the multi-pointed skate of a traditionally wrapped hackle. The fly's action on the water would be light as a feather and bound to attract the trout's attention.

An interesting side note is that Hewitt's skater (for some reason the name spider always stuck with the fly, although you do occasionally hear it referred to as a skater spider too) baffled some of the best fly tiers of the time. They couldn't figure out how he was able to wrap the hackles so compactly to achieve the precise convergence of their tips. Charles Fox reports in his book, *This Wonderful World of Trout*, that in his group of fishing pals Vince Marinaro solved the problem when he realized that Hewitt had to have used unwaxed thread to tie the fly. That may not seem like such a big deal since many of us now use unwaxed thread, but when Hewitt came up with the fly most tiers waxed the thread. Marinaro realized that if you used unwaxed thread, you could wind the hackle at the rear of the fly and then use your thumb and forefinger to jam it together along the hook shank, which compacted it in much the way you might compact spun deer hair on a Muddler head. When you compacted the front hackle in the same way by jamming it toward the rear, the hackle tips met nicely.

The fly could be fished effectively on a dead-drift to rising trout or used to search water that you believed might hold trout, but it was most deadly when danced over the water's surface by holding the rod tip high and skating the fly. Hewitt called it butterfly fishing. The downside to butterfly fishing was that the combination of long stiff hackles and the small size 16 hook made it difficult to actually hook up when you got a strike. The strikes could be vicious, but if you pulled the trigger prematurely, you'd end up missing the hookup. The key was to delay setting the hook for as long as you could stand it. At some point, the seemingly insurmountable difficulties of successfully hooking up when a trout did strike led some fly fishers to use the spider only as a searching tool to locate where the trout were and then come back later in the day and fish the location with a different fly that could more efficiently hook and hold the fish.

Eventually, fly tiers began to put their minds to the hookup difficulties, and it wasn't long before they realized they could simply use a larger hook if they added a bit more hackle. The tiers found that if they added four or five hackle feathers (for odd number hackles the extra one is added to the rear hackle of the fly, which tends to take more of a beating) to size 8, 10, or 12 fine wire, short-shank hooks their spiders performed adequately.

When I got into experimenting with spiders, none of this background was available. We pretty much heard about them on the river and maybe saw a few photos in a book or magazine, but we didn't know anything about compressing the hackle or getting the hackle tips to meet. We just tied oversize hackle on short-shank hooks, and our results were mixed. Sometimes we'd manage to entice a fish into a slashing strike and maybe even catch one, but the fly was acting more like a Fore-and-Aft hackled dry fly than a true spider. Some of that was because we didn't know how to tie the fly, but it was also difficult to find non-webby hackle that was long enough and stiff enough to work on a spider fly.

In addition, our fly fishing seemed to be getting a lot more businesslike. Some of us were guiding, and the emphasis was going more and more toward just catching fish,

A modern spider pattern may have more than two hackles, especially if it's tied on a larger hook. This example, tied on a size 12, Tiemco 921 hook, has three Cree hackles on the rear and two brown hackles on the front. Note that the hackle tips have been lightly cemented together.

The hackle fibers on an older genetic hackle (left) are less dense but stronger, which makes them a better choice for spider patterns. The hackle fibers on the highly evolved genetic hackle (right) are dense, but tend to be thin, curved, and weak.

which meant concentrating on short-line nymphing or dialing in the hatches with precision flies that matched the size, shape, and color of the naturals. Over time we forgot how much of a hoot it was to skate a silver dollar–sized all-hackle dry fly over some flat water and rile up a few trout—even if we didn't land every one of them.

Ed Shenk changed all that for me when I stumbled across a somewhat dated magazine article he'd written about skater spiders. The article detailed how fly fishers in Montana were using large spider patterns to catch large trout. And most important, he revealed the secret of tying the skater spider. That's where I first learned how to compact the hackle and one other very important tip. Shenk recommended that after you wrapped the hackle, you should put a tiny bit of head cement on the tips and press them together. He said that it would stiffen up the hackle a bit more and keep the fly "riding on its tip-toes."

Let's fast-forward about ten years. It's 2008, and I'm up on the famous Spinney Mountain Ranch section of the South Platte River. It's a crisp but quickly warming June morning, and I have three spider flies that I want to test-drive. I tied them on size 12 Tiemco 921 hooks. These hooks feature a 2X short shank made of 1X fine wire. My biggest fear when I was tying the flies was that I wouldn't be able to find suitable hackle. I tried some larger feathers from a new, highly evolved genetic cape, but they weren't quite right. It wasn't that there was too much web, but rather the individual hackle fibers, although quite dense, seemed thin and weak. Clearly the cape had been produced for the smaller feathers that exhibited no web at all and lots of fibers per feather that would result in a bushy, buoyant hackle. It's exactly what you need to tie today's dry-fly patterns, but not what you need to dance a spider over the water's surface.

I finally broke open some older boxes of capes that I hadn't looked at in years and eventually found what turned out to be older genetic hackle that had fewer, but stronger, individual fibers. There was some web on the larger feathers that I would have to use, but that was always part of the game when it came to tying spiders. And besides, I could make up for that with Shenk's technique of cementing the hackle tips together to add extra stiffness. After a bit of experimentation, I decided to use three Cree hackles for the rear and two brown hackles for the front of the fly.

My friend Angus Drummond, a young guide and promising angling photographer who also knows the Spinney Mountain Ranch section of the South Platte as well as anyone, was with me when I broke out the spiders and tied one on the end of my 9-foot leader that was tapered to a 2X tippet. I told him we used to fish spiders years ago, and that I'd been thinking about them and just wanted to try one again. I wasn't surprised when he said that he'd read an article about spiders just a few years ago and thought about tying some himself, but he didn't have the hackle that was required, and he just got busy with other things before he could track down something that might work.

We walked to a nearby riffle where Angus pointed out a few trout holding below the

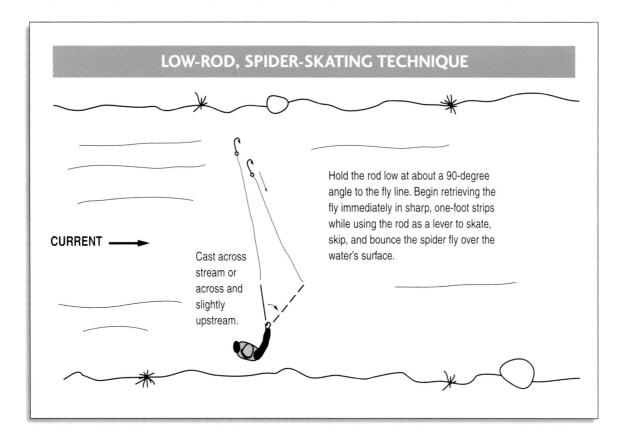

LOW-ROD, SPIDER-SKATING TECHNIQUE

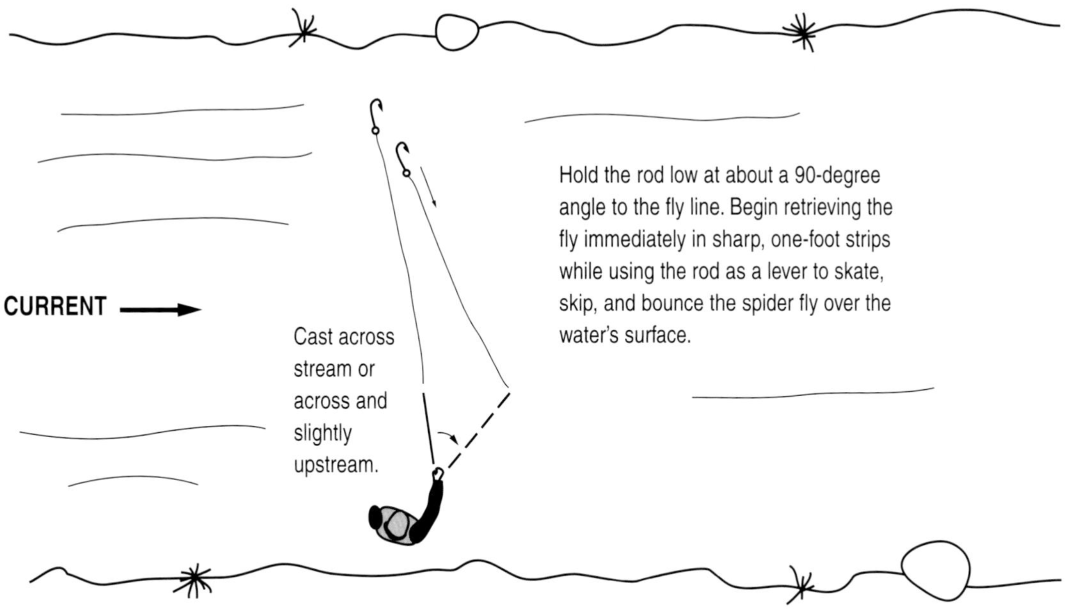
CURRENT
Cast across stream or across and slightly upstream.
Hold the rod low at about a 90-degree angle to the fly line. Begin retrieving the fly immediately in sharp, one-foot strips while using the rod as a lever to skate, skip, and bounce the spider fly over the water's surface.

surface in about two feet of water. "Why don't you give your spider a try on those guys," he said. I greased the entire leader to keep the fly up and dry and made my first cast. Nothing happened. Angus watched the fly and said, "That thing really does float high. No trouble seeing that one for sure." It's the sort of observation you would expect from a guy who guides 130 trips a year on a tailwater that's renowned for its technical trout, and where you seldom use a dry fly larger than size 16. I had cast for about twenty minutes and was just beginning to lose hope when a rainbow trout came out of nowhere and slashed at the fly. A few casts later the same trout followed the fly again but didn't take it.

After that, Angus headed upstream to work a large brown trout he'd spotted the day before. I moved up to the next riffle and kept working the spider. At the previous rif-

Use a desiccant powder to revive a waterlogged spider fly.

fle, I had been experimenting with casting the fly slightly upstream, holding the rod close to the water's surface and trying to skate it by making short retrieves. It quickly became clear that the fly skated better if I didn't point the rod tip directly at it, but rather held it at about a 90-degree angle to the fly. I later practiced a high-stick style of skating the fly by holding the rod high and keeping as much fly line off the water as possible. I found that both techniques worked best if I didn't cast the fly directly upstream or at too much of a downstream-and-across angle where it was harder to control the drag and keep the current from pulling it under.

I was using the high-stick skating technique when another trout attacked the fly, and I struck too soon. I admonished myself to be cool and hold back and immediately cast back to the same spot. The trout then nailed the fly without hesitation, and I was hooked up. A short time later, I released a chunky 15-inch rainbow trout. In the scheme of things, that's not saying much for a river that consistently provides 18-inch-plus trout until you consider that I caught the fish from a heralded high-tech tailwater where most fly fishers never go much larger than a 5X tippet and a size 18 fly. And here I was with my 2X tippet and a dry fly with hackle the size of a fifty-cent piece. The trout had blown up on it like a largemouth bass, and I was admittedly a little proud of myself.

I've caught numerous trout on the spider since then and learned a few more tricks in the process:

1. If the spider gets wet or waterlogged, it's easy to restore it with one of the desiccant powders that are now available.

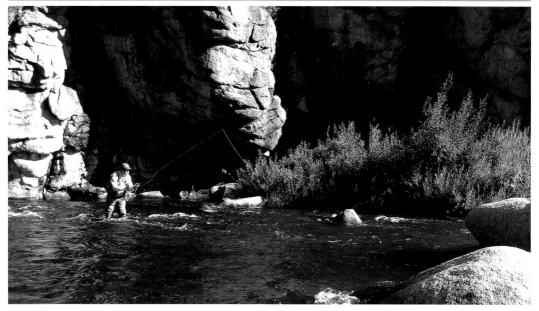

Cast the spider across and downstream and hold as much fly line off the water as possible.

Skate the fly by lifting the rod or drawing it across your body to hop, skip, or skate the fly upstream or across the current.

2. Once in a while, try retrieving the spider as fast as you can all the way back to your position.
3. When you're high-sticking the fly, make it bounce rather than skate for a change of pace.

I've also learned that a big spider is not the easiest fly to cast. You might want to keep the leader to 9 feet or even a little shorter and never go below a 2X or 3X tippet. Although it's possible to fish spiders on a 3-weight or 4-weight rod, a heavier rod makes it easier and is essential if it's windy. Finally if your spider does sink and you can't revive it, you might consider retrieving it below the surface a few times before you switch it out for a nice new one. Odds are you'll discover that it's a killer subsurface fly too.

So there you have it. I've added butterfly fishing to my list of fly-fishing tactics. I like the simplicity and lightness of fishing spiders. They also taught me that there is more to dry-fly fishing than the dead drift. Sometimes action is the attraction. I know I would have caught more and larger trout short-lining nymphs. But fishing spiders strips everything down to a single raw essential. It's all about the strike and the rush. And that, my friend, keeps me coming back to the river.

TRIGGERS

When you begin babbling about how fishing spiders strips everything down to the essentials, you're never very far from thinking about what makes a trout strike a fly in the first place. Match-the-hatch logic informs us that it's all about translating a reasonable facsimile of the natural to an imitation on a hook. The imitation doesn't have to look exactly like the natural, but it should be close to the size, color, and silhouette or shape of the real thing. That's one of the first lessons in Fly Fishing 101, and it behooves us to learn it well. Matching the hatch provides a framework to organize a lot of information that comes to you on the river. And on any given day, the odds favor a fisherman who matches the food that is available to the trout, especially if he has the technical fly-fishing skills to back up his fly.

Somehow the idea of matching the hatch comforts me, and I can say it has accounted for a good many trout on what you might call technical waters. But I have always been fascinated by whatever that spark is that actually makes the trout take a fly in the first place. Sure, match-the-hatch thinking gets you close, but it's hard to believe that a minor adjustment in something like the hue of the dubbing material will make that big a difference. And if indeed it does, could it be that your confidence in the different hue may be what's really responsible? Confidence makes you fish better because you concentrate more and tend to fish a favorite fly pattern longer and with more enthusiasm.

But there are also instances where a new fly-tying material or a different application of a proven material or an altogether different fly design greatly increases a fly's effectiveness. That kind of discovery includes and goes beyond the concrete rationality of matching the hatch and straight to the heart of what ultimately makes a trout take a fly. I call it the trigger. It's that elemental force that some flies possess that seems to induce strikes whether they are designed to match a specific insect or simply serve as an attractor. It's always difficult when it comes down to figuring out what actually triggers the trout

The match-the-hatch philosophy is based on matching the size, color, and shape of the natural, but discovering what triggers a trout to take a fly may not necessarily have anything to do with matching the appearance of the natural.

to take a fly because the relationship of the trigger to the insect you are imitating or a certain behavior of an insect that you are trying to imitate usually isn't direct. The fact is that finding that relationship most often occurs by accident. That's why it's always important to pay attention to your fly tying and fishing accidents and mishaps.

I didn't know anything about triggers when I first got interested in fishing and tying small flies. I just wanted to catch a few trout from the South Platte River, which happened to be a tailwater where most of the insects that the trout fed on were very small. It didn't take long for me to understand that if I wanted to catch them, I'd have to learn to tie small flies to match the naturals. After I'd been tying small flies for a number of years, I realized that a small fly's

inherent simplicity made it an ideal laboratory for the study of triggers. Most small fly patterns are pretty basic ties because it's crucial to keep the bulk down due to their size. There just isn't much room to tie a bunch of extraneous materials on the hook. That reduces you to the essentials, which gets you closer to the realm of triggers if only because a small fly is less complicated and has fewer variables to examine.

Nonetheless finding a trigger is an esoteric business that often doesn't follow logically from observation. More than anything, it's important to not fall into a silver bullet kind of mentality. Finding a trigger isn't going to mean you can throw out your fly box and just start catching trout on every cast, everywhere you go. But it does mean that under a certain set of reproducible conditions a fly that incorporates the trigger will perform quite well. You might also consider the difficulty of stumbling onto a real trigger. My mother was always fond of saying you may have a lot of acquaintances in your life, but count yourself lucky if you make one or two real friends. In a lot of ways, discovering a trigger is a bit like making a real friend.

So what follows are a few thoughts and examples of what I've learned to recognize as pathways that could lead to the discovery of triggers, especially in regards to small flies, although I have come to believe that many of these ideas can be applied to any size fly. If you have read my book, *Tying Small Flies*, you'll see that I have updated some of my commentary on triggers that appeared there. I've also included some new ideas and different combinations of older ideas. The point is that you don't really get that many chances to discover real triggers. It's a lot like chasing shadows, and if you think you're on the track of one, it's really important to stick with it, refine it, and enjoy it.

The Blue Fly

You may remember coming across a little blue midge imitation in *Tying Small Flies* that my friend Stan Benton originated. I think he called it Stan's Blue Midge. That's not a flashy catch-a-fly-fisherman name like you see professional fly tiers putting on patterns nowadays, but Stan's little midge is probably still the closest I've seen to a pure trigger. The tie is simple—blue Krystal Flash wrapped around the hook shank with blue Arizona Yarn for a thorax.

Stan said he came up with the pattern after he read a summary of a paper by R. M.

Ginetz and P. A. Larkin titled, "Choice of Colors of Food Items by Rainbow Trout." It appeared in the *Journal of Fisheries Board of Canada* in the early 1970s.

The authors found that hatchery rainbow trout that had only been fed reddish-brown pellets could distinguish between salmon eggs that were dyed seven different colors and preferred certain colors over others. Under normal daylight conditions, they liked blue, red, black, orange, brown, yellow, and green in that order of preference when the eggs were presented against a pale blue-green background.

The researchers found that when they varied the light intensity and background color in some cases the trout's preference could be explained by the greater contrast between the egg and a given background, but they still seemed to have consistent preferences for certain colors under all conditions and especially in dim light. But here's the clincher. The trout selected blue eggs over eggs of other colors under normal light conditions even when they were placed against a blue background. This indicates that they could discriminate between what could only have been very slight differences in the shades of blue between the background and the eggs, but even more interesting was that they still preferred the blue egg even though it must have been more difficult to detect.

Stan's Blue Midge seemed to strike a nerve when it appeared in *Tying Small Flies*. Since the book was published in 2004, I have corresponded with numerous fly fishers and fly tiers who all wanted to talk about and understand their success with blue flies. Stan had made the point when he first showed me the Blue Midge that it clearly

Stan's Blue Midge has inspired numerous other blue midge patterns—(from left) the Deep Blue Poison Tung, GR-Blue Bead Midge, and Little Blue Fly.

worked best in the winter and early spring, but he didn't have any idea why that would be true. Surprisingly many of the correspondents agreed that their renditions of blue flies also seemed most effective during the winter, although several mentioned success with the fly year-round.

Our discussions moved quickly to why a blue fly is effective at all since there aren't a lot of aquatic insects or other trout foods that are blue. One correspondent suggested that since the color blue is on the short wavelength side of the visible spectrum a blue fly would continue to look blue at a greater water depth, whereas a red fly, which has a longer wavelength, would appear black or dark because its color would have been absorbed at a shallower depth. We agreed that's great science, but it didn't explain why Stan's Midge was deadly in a foot or two of clear water where a red fly would still be red. Other fly fishers posited that

Stan's Blue Midge doesn't match a natural, but something about the fly triggers strikes.

the fly was more effective in winter because the water was clearer and the lower angle of the sun's light might somehow cause the color blue to brighten or light up more than other colors. When the day was done, though, we all agreed that we couldn't explain with any current fly-fishing logic why the fly works. It is interesting to contemplate, though, that match-the-hatch principles, at least in terms of color, may not always apply to triggers. Nonetheless it's still all conjecture as far as I can tell, which means it's still among the sweetest fly-fishing mysteries I know.

GR-BLUE BEAD MIDGE

Hook:	Tiemco 2488, size 18–20
Thread:	Black Gudebrod 10/0
Rib:	UTC extra small silver wire
Thorax:	Black Nature's Spirit Fine Natural Dubbing
Bead:	Cobalt blue Glass Seed Bead from Mill Hill

CHARLIE CRAVEN'S DEEP BLUE POISON TUNG

Hook:	Tiemco 2488, sizes 16–24
Thread:	Gray 8/0 Uni-Thread
Rib:	Blue Lagartun wire (fine)
Thorax:	Gray UV Ice Dub
Bead:	2-mm silver-colored tungsten

DAN QUATRO'S LITTLE BLUE FLY

Hook:	Daiichi 1130, sizes 18–24
Thread:	Light Blue 8/0
Rib:	Pearl Midge Rainbow Flash
Thorax:	Blue Dun or Cream Beaver dubbing—mix in a touch of Antron if you like
Bead:	Spirit River X-Small silver glass bead

In honor of that mystery, I offer blue fly pattern recipes and commentary from Glenn Weisner, Charlie Craven, and Dan Quatro.

Weisner and Wayne Samson, his fishing pal and business partner at Glenn River Fly Co. Ltd., have tested the Blue Bead Midge on a variety of spring creeks in Ohio, Wisconsin, Minnesota, Montana, and Pennsylvania. At one point, Weisner tested the fly with twelve different colored glass beads that were obtained from the same distributor and were the same size as the cobalt blue bead. The hook size, thread, dubbing, ribbing, and thorax were unchanged. The flies were fished on an 18-inch dropper behind a sizeable Elk Hair Caddis. Each fly was drifted through the same stretch of water ten times.

"The results were staggering," Weisner said. "The cobalt blue glass bead midge was eaten nine out of ten times. A black glass bead was second best with five takes!"

Weisner believes the cobalt blue bead and the segmentation provided by the fly's silver ribbing are crucial to its success. He recommends fishing the fly by itself in the surface film or using it as the down fly in a two-fly dropper system with a highly visible dry fly, such as the Elk Hair Caddis used in the test.

Charlie said that he was amazed the fussy trout on Colorado's South Platte River would dart a couple of feet out of their feeding lanes to take this fly. "You don't know how unusual that is," Charlie exclaimed.

Dan says his Little Blue Fly is pretty straightforward. "When it works, it works really well," he said.

Oversize Thorax

Fly tiers are taught that their flies should have the right proportions. It's nice to have everything neat and tidy and a fly that sort of looks like the natural. That's especially true if you're tying for other fly tiers. If you want to get one up on the trout, try oversizing the thorax area on your immature aquatic insect imitations. I first reported the oversize thorax connection in *Tying Small Flies* in regards to midge pupae and a fly called the WD-40. I now believe you'll increase the effectiveness of many nymph and pupa imitations by just oversizing the thorax. If you like experimenting with pattern design, consider increasing the size of the thorax by two or more times what you consider the normal proportion. Some of my midge pupa imitations now have thoraxes that take up as much as half the hook!

Unlike the blue midge fly patterns, I think match-the-hatch logic does apply to the fat thorax trigger. Just consider the moment a pupa or nymph begins getting out of the nymphal or pupal shuck. The wing pads are already enormous because they are fully developed and will be unfolding momentarily.

A nymph imitation tied with an oversize thorax may not have the right proportions, but it may have a better chance of triggering a strike.

In addition, the abdomen of the insect is scrunching up toward the top of the shuck in an effort to get out. With all that, the thorax is bound to look oversized. And that could be a strong visual signal to trout. Why not make the visual signal on your imitation even stronger by forgetting the traditional approach to proportions and making the thorax larger so it stands out even more? It's worth a shot.

Segmentation

Strongly emphasized segmentation sells a fly pattern to trout. This is especially true for midge larvae and midge pupae. It took me a while to understand why strongly emphasized segmentation might be a trigger because when I collected samples of immature aquatic insects I wasn't always able to discern strongly contrasting segmentation. That all changed one day when I noticed that, depending on how the light hit the insect, its segmentation could go from barely discernable to highly visible. I now think that, depending on the light, about 80 to 90 percent of the larvae, pupae, and nymphs I collect display highly visible segmentation. It only makes sense that it would be an important visual cue to the trout and under the right light conditions could be an almost overwhelming visual cue.

The key to finding the segmentation trigger for fly patterns is to experiment with materials. Two contrasting colors of wire wrapped around the hook shank may do it. Thread wrapped over latex tubing that has been slipped over the hook shank really emphasizes segmentation. For smaller flies, microtubing wrapped around the hook shank will give good results. Goose biot probably comes the closest to actually imitating the way segmentation appears on the natural, and stripped quill is a close second. Both of these natural materials are always near the top of my list when I try to emphasize segmentation on a new fly pattern. I've also had success by simply ribbing a thread-bodied fly with a fine wire or thread rib of a different color.

I should conclude by saying that this is one trigger where you'll want to begin by using your match-the-hatch skills to match the main color of the natural's abdomen and then use a material for the rib that contrasts from the main color to emphasize the segmentation. And finally, don't forget the lesson of the oversized thorax—it doesn't hurt to overemphasize segmentation through the use of highly contrasting colors for the main body color and rib.

Shucks

A number of years ago, I got it into my head that the color of the nymphal or pupal shuck might be a trigger. That led to an experiment where I tried to match the color of the shucks of various hatches. At the time I thought I was on the right track to finding a viable trigger especially for midges. I even mentioned in *Tying Small Flies* that matching shuck color seemed to improve the effectiveness of some of my midge patterns. It all sort of made sense, but as time went by I ultimately found that, unfortunately, the trout disagreed.

During the process, I did, however, find that the trout seemed to appreciate a dark amber Antron shuck regardless of the color of the shuck of whatever insect was hatching. Having made that observation, I noted that

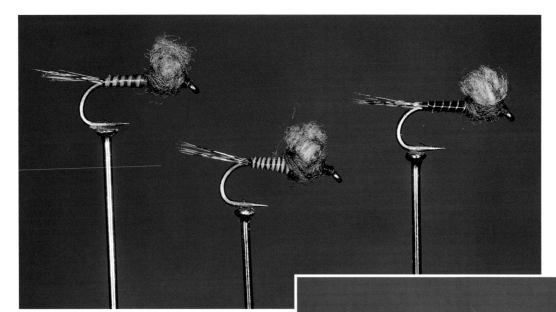

Segmentation is an important trigger. Different tying materials give different segmentation effects—(from left) goose biot, stripped quill, and wire over a thread body.

historically a number of successful fly pat-terns such as the Adams and Prince Nymph have employed brown tailing material, which might not have been a coincidence. It might be that the tiers noticed that flies with a brown tailing material seemed more effec-tive. It's easy to generalize this kind of obser-vation. But then again you might consider adding amber-colored Antron tails or shucks on some of your nymph or pupa imitations, if only to see what happens.

FLASH & ACTION
Everything changed when compact, flashy Mylar-type products such as Flashabou and Krystal Flash became available to those of us who like tying small flies. It didn't take too many test sessions on the river to realize that

An amber Antron tail or shuck may increase a fly's effectiveness.

flash in a small fly pattern triggered strikes. Most of us reasoned that the flash made a fly more visible, and those of us who had spent any time watching midges hatch in our ob-servation aquariums at home also noted the way a midge pupa flashes when it fills its shuck with air (or whatever it fills with) on the way to the surface or when suspended in the surface film. That flash at emergence was a dinner bell to the trout. Pearlescent Mylar was as close to imitating that flashy trigger as you could get without stringing a natural to your hook. The results were nothing short of phenomenal.

It's been several decades since those heady days of discovery, but synthetic flash added to a small fly imitation is still one of the purest triggers you can find. No one doubts that the flash helps the trout find a small fly in the water, but it's also possible that the flash represents movement or action to the trout. If that's true, it might not hurt to actively fish nymph or pupa imitations. It took me several seasons before I acted on the idea, though, because I reasoned that a pupa or nymph dead-drifted in the current moved the fly enough to keep it active and flashing.

Then one day I met up with my friend Hobie Ragland on the South Platte River. Although it was a cold January day with air temperatures hovering around 30 degrees, trout were porpoising and bulging to emerging midge pupae. We were both dead drifting pupa imitations in hopes of getting a strike, but Hobie was doing a lot better than I was. I finally asked him what he was doing that was different. "It might be that I'm lifting the fly a bit at the end of the drift." I

watched his next drift, and sure enough toward the end of it he slowly lifted the fly. Further observation revealed that sometimes he lifted the fly just a few inches and then dropped the rod tip. Other times he made a slow steady lift until the fly came all the way to the surface. The lifts resulted in strikes with a predictable regularity.

Let's just say that was enough proof for me, and for the past four or five years I've been "activating" my tiny flies, and for that matter most of my other flies, whenever a dead drift doesn't work. And, yes, I'd call it a trigger. And just think if there was ever a bastion of the dead drift, it had to have been small flies. (See chapter 3 for more ideas on fishing an active fly.)

Dry flies that sink, the metaphysics of what triggers a trout to take an artificial fly, an old dry fly from the 1920s that doesn't imitate anything, but still catches fish. These aren't exactly topics on the leading edge of fly-fishing thought and technology. And that's fine with me. It's always been the little backwaters, detours, oddities, and weirdness that keep me coming back to the river. And I still always wonder what the trout are up to. . . .

REFERENCES AND BOOKS OF INTEREST

Bates Jr., Joseph D. *Streamer Fly Tying and Fishing*. Harrisburg, PA: The Stackpole Company, 1966.

Bergman, Ray. *Trout*. New York: Alfred A. Knopf, 1949.

Best, A. K. *Production Fly Tying*. Boulder, CO: Pruett Publishing Company, 2003.

Craven, Charlie. *Charlie Craven's Basic Fly Tying*. New Cumberland, PA: Headwater Books, 2008.

Dennis, Jack. *Tying Flies with Jack Dennis and Friends*. Jackson, WY: Snake River Books, 1993.

Engle, Ed. *Fly Fishing the Tailwaters*. Harrisburg, PA: Stackpole Books, 1991.

———. *Tying Small Flies*. Mechanicsburg, PA: Stackpole Books, 2004.

———. *Fishing Small Flies*. Mechanicsburg, PA: Stackpole Books, 2005.

Fox, Charles K. *The Wonderful World of Trout*. Rockville Centre, NY: Freshet Press, 1971.

Hughes, Dave. *Wet Flies: Tying and Fishing Soft-Hackles, Winged and Wingless Wets, and Fuzzy Nymphs*. Mechanicsburg, PA: Stackpole Books, 1995.

Humphreys, Joe. *Joe Humphreys's Trout Tactics*. Harrisburg, PA: Stackpole Books, 1981.

Kageyama, Colin J. *What Fish See: Understanding Optics and Color Shifts for Designing Lures and Flies*. Portland, OR: Frank Amato Publications, 1999.

LaBranche, George M. L. *The Dry Fly and Fast Water and The Salmon and the Dry Fly*. New York: Charles Scribner's Sons, 1951.

LaFontaine, Gary. *Caddisflies*. New York: Lyons & Burford, 1981.

———. *The Dry Fly: New Angles*. Helena, MT: Greycliff Publishing, 1990.

Lawson, Mike. *Spring Creeks*. Mechanicsburg, PA: Stackpole Books, 2003.

Migel, J. Michael, and Leonard M. Wright Jr., eds. *The Masters on the Nymph*. Guilford, CT: Globe Pequot Press, 2002.

Proper, Datus. *What the Trout Said*. New York: Lyons & Burford, 1989.

Shenk, Ed. "The Skater Spider," *Fly Fisherman* 29, No. 2 (March 1988).

INDEX

Page numbers in italics indicate illustrations.

beaver ponds, 150–56, *151*
    connector streams, *153*
    cycle, 150–51
    fly patterns for, 154–55
    targeting larger trout on, 155–56
    using a systems approach when fishing, 152–54
    using topographical maps to find, 149–50
Benton, Stan, 172–73
Best, A. K., 39, 40, 87–88
Betts, John, vi
Byford, Dan, 40

casting techniques
    across-and-downstream, *46*, 72, *73*
    across-and-upstream, 72, *73*
    for beaver ponds, *152*, 152–54
    check, *102*
    down-and-dirty, 29
    downstream-and-across reach, 103, *103*
    downstream mend, *46*
    drag-and-nag, 27, *27*
    grass, *74*
    high-sticking streamer, *119*, 119–22
    high-stick spider skating, 168, *169*
    hopper-dropper, 159
    lowering rod tip and using strip strike, *47*
    mousing, 84–86
    parachute, *101*
    plop-and-drop, 25, *25*
    quartering across-and-downstream, *43*, 44
    reach, *100*
    same-side downstream, *81*
    slap-and-dap, *26*, 26–27
    for small streams, 136–40, *137*

speed of the swing, 44–45
spider-skating, 166, *167*
splash-and-crash, *24*, 24–25
sudden inch, *28*, 29
for trout in difficult lies, 99–104
upstream, *99*
upstream mend, 45
using spent spinners, *33, 34*
for wild meadow streams, *72*, 72–74, *73, 74, 75, 76*
see also tight-line techniques
"Choice of Colors of Food Items by Rainbow Trout" (paper), 172
Craven, Charlie, 175

Drummond, Angus, 167–68
Dry Fly and Fast Water, The (LaBranche), 23

Eng, Wayne, 89

Fishing Small Flies (Engle), 163
Flashabou, 177
fly-fishing methods, vi–vii
    active fly, 23–29
    butterfly, 165
    for difficult trout, 89–104
    drag-free drift, vi
    high water, 105–30
    matching the hatch, vi, *21, 22,* 170
    wild meadow stream, 70–78
    see also casting techniques; nymphing and nymphing techniques; tight-line techniques
fly patterns
    Adams, 36, 141
    Adams Parachute, 155

for beaver ponds, 154–55
Bivisible, *29*, 30, 32, 61
blue, 172–75
Blue Bead Midge, 175
Brassie, 38, 141
Burlap Fly, *113*, 113–14
CDC Comparadun, *91*
CDC Dunn, 155
Chamois Leech, *113*, 114
Convertible, *31*, 32, 129
Copper John, 110, 112
Deep Blue Poison Tung, *173, 174*
deer-hair beetle, *163*
deer-hair mouse, 64, *84*
deer-hair style grasshopper, 63–64
for difficult trout situations, *91*
dry, tight-line techniques for, 59–66
Elk Hair Caddis, 36, 58, 61, 66, 70, 133, 141, 163,
    163
flash in, 177–78
fluorescent, 126
Gold-Ribbed Hare's Ear, 38, 110, 112, *112*, 141
grasshopper, 141, *162*
GR-Blue Bead Midge, *173, 174*
Griffith's Gnat, 36, 155
Gunni Special, *125*, 126
hackled, *91*
hackles used in, *166*
hairwing Comparadun, *91*
for high off-color water, 129–30
House and Lot, 133
Ishiwata's Busted Hopper, 160, *161*
lacquered-thread ant, *163*
LaFontaine Emergent Sparkle Caddisfly Pupa, *52*
Lawson's Wet Hopper, 160
Lime Trude, 141
Little Blue Fly, *173, 174*
Marabou Leech, 155
Mickey Finn, 155
modern spider, *165*
Muddler Minnow, *50*, 51, 162
for muddy water, 124–27
Neversink Skater, 164–65
nymph with oversize thorax, *175*
for off-color water, 110–14
oversizing the thorax of, 175–76
parachute with dubbed body, *91*

Parachute Hare's Ear, *71*, 131, 141
parachute with quill body, *91*
Pheasant Tail, 38, *112*, 141
Prince Nymph, 38, 52, 110, 112, *112*, 141
Rio Grande King Trude, 133, 141
Royal Coachman, 20, 32, 141
Royal Coachman Trude, 20–21, 133, 141
Royal Wulff, 32, 36, 66, 133
Rubber Band Fly, 113, *113*
segmented, 176, *177*
shuck color of, 176–77, *177*
sinking dry, 157–63
for small streams, 133, 141, *142*
soft-hackle wet, 42, *42*
spent spinner, *32, 33, 34, 97*
spider, 164–70, *168*
Standard Royal Coachman, 133
Stan's Blue Midge, 172–73, *173*
Stimulator, 58, 61, 66, 70, 129, 141
streamer, 40–41, *51, 123*, 155
streamer with Homer Rhode loop knot, *52*
Takahaski's Drowned Hopper, 160, *161*
for tight liners, 50–52
trigger, 170–77
for trout in difficult lies, 100
Turck's Tarantula, 129, *129*
using Homer Rhode loop knot when tying, 52
WD-40, 175
weighted streamer, *80*
for wild meadow streams, 70–71
Woolly Bugger, 40, *50*, 70, *120*, 121, 155
Yellow Stimulator, 133
Zonker, 40, 41, *41, 125*, 155
Zuddler, *120*, 121, *125*
fly patterns, attractor, 19–23
   Adams, 36
   Bivisible, *29*, 30, 32
   Brassie, 38
   casting techniques for, 23–29
   CDC Blue-Winged Olive, 37, *37*
   color of, 35–36
   Compardun, 36
   Convertible, *31*, 32
   Elk Hair Caddis, 36
   Gold-Ribbed Hare's Ear, 38
   Griffith's Gnat, 36
   H & L Variants, 20

Hare's Ear Soft Hackle, 35
Lime-Bodied Coachmen, 20
match-the-hatch, *21, 22,* 36–37
Pheasant Tail, 38
Prince Nymph, 38
Royal Coachman, 20, 32
Royal Coachman Trude, 20–21
Royal Wulff, 32, 36
San Juan Worm, 38
for specific water types, 29–36, *30*
spent spinner, *32, 33, 34*
subsurface, 37–38
Fothergill, Chuck, 6, 8, 16
Fox, Charles, 164
Furimsky, Ben, 127

Gierach, John, 132
grills, campfire, 19–20

hackles, *166*
hatches, 92–99
multiple, various stages of, 93–98
Hewitt, Edward R., 87, 164, 165
Hidy, Pete, 57
high water, 105–7, *116, 117*
dry flies for off-color, 129–30
early-season snowmelt, 107–8
finding trout in, *118*
fishing, *106*
flies that trout can see in muddy, 124–27
high-sticking streamer technique for, 119–22
muddy, 122–24
mud line, *108,* 108–9, *109*
nymphing techniques for, 114–19, *115*
off-color, 108–14, *111*
tailwater, *127,* 127–29
Hill, Roger, 22
Hughes, Dave, 56

insects, *171*
grasshoppers, *160*
multiple hatches of, 92–99
Tricos, *93, 95*
Trico spinner, *158*

Kageyama, Colin, filter studies, 124–26
Kreh, Lefty, 6

Krystal Flash, 177

LaBranche, George, 23
LaFontaine, Gary, 52
Lawson, Mike, 36
Leisenring, Jim, 56
lifts
Hidy Subsurface Swing, 56–58, *57*
induced take, 56
Leisenring, 56, 58

maps, topographical, *145,* 145–50, *147, 148, 149*
computer based, 146
Marinaro, Vince, 164
Masters on the Nymph, The (Migel and Wright, ed.), 6
Matching the Hatch (Schwiebert), 89
meadow streams, *71, 83, 85*
casting techniques for, 72–74
characteristics of, 79–82
covering all the water, 76
description of, 67
drops, *75*
inside of the bend tactics, *82*
mousing technique for, 84–86
night fishing, 84–86
seasonal variations in, 82–83
streamer tactics for, 77–82
types of, 67–70, *68, 69*
wild, fishing, 70–78

navigational tools, *150*
night fishing, 84–86
nymphing and nymphing techniques, 1–6
Czech, 10
detecting strikes, 8–10, 16–18
European, 18
Fothergill, 6–8, *7*
high water, 114–19, *115*
lateral line, developing your, 12–13
long-line, *12*
short-line, 104, *104, 116*
short-line dead-drift, *2,* 2–6, *3,* 13–16, *14, 15, 17,* 110
strike indicators, 10–13
suspension rig vs. bottom-bounce rig, *13*
tight-line, 8–10, *9*
water tension cast, *4,* 4–6, *5*

Price, Mike, 134, 137

Quatro, Dan, 175

Ragland, Hobie, 178
Richards, Carl, 89
riseforms, *89, 90,* 91–92, 94, *94,* 97, 98, *98*

Samson, Wayne, 175
Sanchez, Scott, 32
Sawyer, Frank, 56
Schwiebert, Ernest, 89
Selective Trout (Swisher and Richards), 89
Shenk, Ed, 166
Small Stream Stress Index (SSSI), 142–43
streamers, high-sticking, *119,* 119–21
   tackle for, 121–22
streams, small, 131–34, *138, 139, 140, 144*
   basics, 134–40
   catching larger trout on, 143–45
   fly patterns for, 133, 141
   hiding cover in, 134–35, *135, 136*
   prime habitat in, *136*
   streakers, 135–37
   tackle for, 140–43, *141*
   using topographical maps to find, 145–50
Streit, Jackson, 84
strike indicators
   buoyant, 10–13, *11*
   non-buoyant, *11*
strikes, detecting, 8–10
   through the line, 12–13
   when high-sticking a short line, 16–18
Swisher, Doug, 89

Tellin, Dana, 41
This Wonderful World of Trout (Fox), 164
tight-line techniques, 39–42
   advanced subsurface, 53–58
   dapping, *59,* 59–60
   downstream mend, *53,* 53–54
   drag free, skitter-swing, and drown, 58–59
   dry fly, 58–59

full sinking lines, 49–50
greased-line, *54,* 54–56
high-sticking dry fly, 59–66, *61, 62, 63*
keeping fly near bottom, *49*
lifts, 56–58
loch-style high-sticking, *65,* 65–66, *66*
retrieve styles, 48, *48*
sink-tip lines, 48–50
stack mend, 55, *55*
strip, strip, wiggle, wiggle, 54, 84
subsurface, 42–48, *43, 44, 45, 46, 47*
tackle for, 50–52
two streamers, 54
waking fly, 63–65, *64*
weighted or unweighted flies, 48–49
triggers, 170–77
   blue fly patterns, 172–75
   finding, 171–72
   flash, 177–78
   oversize thorax, 175–76
   segmentation, 176
   shucks, 176–77
trout, *78, 88, 109, 133, 155, 156, 158*
   brook, *20*
   difficult, definition of, 88–89
   in difficult lies, 99–104
   feeding behavior, *96,* 98–99
   finding high-water, *118*
   riseforms, *89, 90,* 91–92, 94, *94, 97,* 98, *98*
   selective feeding, 89–92
   slamming a streamer, *66*
   in small streams, 134–40
Tying Small Flies (Engle), 172, 175, 176

water
   attractor fly patterns for specific types of, 29–36
   reading, 137–38
   see also high water
Weisner, Glenn, 175
Wet Flies (Hughes), 56
What Trout See (Kageyama), 124
worms, aquatic, *111, 128*